HAMLYN ALL COLOUR
QUICK & EASY
COOKBOOK

HAMLYN ALL COLOUR
QUICK & EASY
COOKBOOK

HAMLYN

Front cover shows, clockwise from top right:
Chocolate Mousse (237), *Pan-fried Danish Eggs and Bacon* (201),
Chinese Stuffed Avocado (1), *Arctic Chicken with Prawns* (89)

Title page shows, clockwise from top right: *Sole Normandie* (65),
Camembert Puffs with Fruit Conserve (219), *Cider Pears with
Passion Fruit* (256), *Steak with Peppercorn Sauce* (109)

Back cover shows, clockwise from top right:
Green and Gold Salad (169), *Herby Chicken Soup* (33),
Asparagus with Lemon Butter (145), *Pasta with Almonds* (221)

Published in 1990 by
The Hamlyn Publishing Group Limited
a division of The Octopus Publishing Group
Michelin House, 81 Fulham Road, London SW3 6RB
Copyright © The Hamlyn Publishing Group Limited 1990

Line drawings by Lorna Turpin

ISBN 0 600 56993 4

Produced by Mandarin Offset
Printed in Hong Kong

Contents

Useful Facts and Figures

Notes on metrication

In this book quantities are given in metric and Imperial measures. Exact conversion from Imperial to metric measures does not usually give very convenient working quantities and so the metric measures have been rounded off into units of 25 grams. The table below shows the recommended equivalents.

Ounces	Approx g to nearest whole figure	Recommended conversion to nearest unit of 25	Ounces	Approx g to nearest whole figure	Recommended conversion to nearest unit of 25
1	28	25	9	255	250
2	57	50	10	283	275
3	85	75	11	312	300
4	113	100	12	340	350
5	142	150	13	368	375
6	170	175	14	396	400
7	198	200	15	425	425
8	227	225	16 (1 lb) 454		450

Note: When converting quantities over 16 oz first add the appropriate figures in the centre column, then adjust to the nearest unit of 25. As a general guide, 1 kg (1000 g) equals 2.2 lb or about 2 lb 3 oz. This method of conversion gives good results in nearly all cases, although in certain pastry and cake recipes a more accurate conversion is necessary to produce a balanced recipe.

Liquid measures

The millilitre has been used in this book and the following table gives a few examples.

Imperial	Approx ml to nearest whole figure	Recommended ml	Imperial	Approx ml to nearest whole figure	Recommended ml
$\frac{1}{4}$	142	150 ml	1 pint	567	600 ml
$\frac{1}{2}$	283	300 ml	1½ pints	851	900 ml
$\frac{3}{4}$	425	450 ml	1¾ pints	992	1000 ml (1 litre)

Spoon measures All spoon measures given in this book are level unless otherwise stated.

Can sizes At present, cans are marked with the exact (usually to the nearest whole number) metric equivalent of the Imperial weight of the contents, so we have followed this practice when giving can sizes.

Oven temperatures

The table below gives recommended equivalents.

	°C	°F	Gas Mark		°C	°F	Gas Mark
Very cool	110	225	¼	Moderately hot	190	375	5
	120	250	½		200	400	6
Cool	140	275	1	Hot	220	425	7
	150	300	2		230	450	8
Moderate	160	325	3	Very Hot	240	475	9
	180	350	4				

Notes for American and Australian users

In America the 8-fl oz measuring cup is used. In Australia metric measures are now used in conjunction with the standard 250-ml measuring cup. The Imperial pint, used in Britain and Australia, is 20 fl oz, while the American pint is 16 fl oz. It is important to remember that the Australian tablespoon differs from both the British and American tablespoons; the table below gives a comparison. The British standard tablespoon, which has been used throughout this book, holds 17.7 ml, the American 14.2 ml, and the Australian 20 ml. A teaspoon holds approximately 5 ml in all three countries.

British	American	Australian
1 teaspoon	1 teaspoon	1 teaspoon
1 tablespoon	1 tablespoon	1 tablespoon
2 tablespoons	3 tablespoons	2 tablespoons
3½ tablespoons	4 tablespoons	3 tablespoons
4 tablespoons	5 tablespoons	3½ tablespoons

An Imperial/American guide to solid and liquid measures

Imperial	American	Imperial	American
Solid measures		**Liquid measures**	
1 lb butter or margarine	2 cups	¼ pint liquid	⅔ cup liquid
1 lb flour	4 cups	½ pint	1¼ cups
1 lb granulated or caster sugar	2 cups	¾ pint	2 cups
1 lb icing sugar	3 cups	1 pint	2½ cups
8 oz rice	1 cup	1½ pints	3¾ cups
		2 pints	5 cups (2½ pints)

Note: When making any of the recipes in this book, only follow one set of measures as they are not interchangeable.

Introduction

The Hamlyn All Colour Quick and Easy Cookbook is certain to become a valuable part of every busy cook's kitchen. Over 270 tempting recipes, suitable for all occasions, have been selected for the ease and speed of their preparation and cooking. Even the most impressive main courses and desserts take less than an hour to make, and many of the recipes can be on the table in under half an hour. if a recipe does require marinating or chilling, it is noted at the start, so you can plan ahead. As an added bonus, many of these recipes give ideas for advance preparation to make life easier at mealtimes.

This book has been carefully devised with the busy cook in mind. A colour photograph of each recipe illustrates the finished result at a glance. Every recipe also includes the number of servings and the preparation and cooking time, as well as the calorific value, making healthy and well-balanced menu planning simple. The colour coded strip that runs down the edge of each page makes it easy to identify the chapters. Cook's Tips offer time-saving shortcuts, serving suggestions, alternative ingredients or helpful information about any slightly unusual techniques or ingredients. You will also find lots of ideas to make the most of convenience foods in your storecupboard or refrigerator.

This book can help the busy cook discover how to make an impact without a lot of effort. Sometimes it is a matter of trying out unusual combinations, such as Mackerel with Cherries,

New Potatoes with Fennel and Mint or Mango-stuffed Apples. Or a traditional recipe can be simplified, like using cream cheese instead of confectioner's custard for the filling of the French-style Strawberry Flan.

Often the most satisfying meals are elegant in their simplicity. Quickly cooked steak with a cream and peppercorn sauce couldn't be easier, but it seems impressive. Desserts always make a meal special and many dishes can be quickly made. For instance, Chocolate Pots with Cherry Brandy take only about ten minutes to prepare and cook, and you can certainly find five minutes to prepare Fresh Fruit Snow. A salad served as a starter eliminates the need for another salad course, and you will find many appealing ones in this book.

A minute spent on presentation can make all the difference in the appearance of food. A sprig of fresh herbs, a few celery leaves or a twisted lemon slice as a garnish can lift a dish above the ordinary, or swirl in a spoonful of cream or yogurt before serving a soup. Each chapter has dozens of simple ideas to add the finishing touch to meals.

The Hamlyn All Colour Quick and Easy Cookbook is a comprehensive recipe collection. It includes a broad selection, from family favourites to classic dishes guaranteed to impress at dinner parties, all designed to streamline food preparation and give the busy cook more time to relax with family and friends.

Starters

First impressions count and you are certain to get any meal off to a good beginning with this selection of starters. Use the first course to stimulate your guests' appetites and increase their anticipation of the food to follow. Choose the starter after planning the main course, so it has different flavours and textures, but at the same time complements it.

1 | Chinese Stuffed Avocado

Preparation time
30 minutes

Serves 6

Calories
247 per portion

You will need
3 avocados
1 small lemon wedge
parsley sprigs to garnish
thinly sliced brown bread and
 butter to serve (optional)

For the filling
1 x 200-g / 7-oz can tuna fish,
 drained and flaked
75 g / 3 oz bean-sprouts, chopped
1 carrot, grated
1 tablespoon chopped fresh
 parsley
1 stick celery, finely chopped
pinch ground ginger
pinch sugar
3 tablespoons mayonnaise
salt and pepper

Halve and stone the avocados, then wipe the cut surfaces with lemon juice.

To make the filling, mix all the ingredients together. Equally divide the filling between the avocado halves.

Arrange on individual plates. Garnish with sprigs of parsley and serve with brown bread and butter on a separate plate, if liked.

2 | Parma Ham with Avocado

Preparation time
10 minutes

Serve 4

Calories
138 per portion

You will need
2 ripe avocados
12 slices Parma ham, about
 175 g / 6 oz

For the dressing
2 tablespoons olive oil
2 teaspoons lemon juice
2 garlic cloves, peeled and
 crushed
4 teaspoons chopped fresh
 parsley
salt and pepper

Halve, stone and peel the avocados, then cut each half into 3 thick slices.

Wrap each slice of ham around a slice of avocado. Arrange on individual plates or a serving dish.

To make the dressing, place all the ingredients in a jar and shake well to mix. Pour the dressing over the avocado to serve.

Cook's Tip

An avocado is ready to eat when it yields just a little if you gently squeeze it in the palm of your hand.

Cook's Tip

To prepare the avocado slices wrapped in ham in advance, brush each slice with lemon juice. This prevents the avocado flesh turning brown. The dressing will keep for up to 1 week in the refrigerator.

3 | *Avocado and Fruit Cocktails with Blue Cheese Dressing*

Preparation time
10 minutes

Makes 4

Calories
240 per portion

You will need
1 avocado, peeled, stoned and diced
1 mango, peeled, stoned and diced
2 grapefruit, peeled and segmented

For the dressing
2 tablespoons mayonnaise
1 tablespoon oil
2 teaspoons white wine vinegar
salt and pepper
50 g / 2 oz blue cheese

To make the blue cheese dressing, mix together the mayonnaise, oil, vinegar and salt and pepper to taste. Grate or crumble in the blue cheese and mix well.

Put the avocado, mango and grapefruit in a bowl. Pour in the dressing, toss lightly, then divide between four dishes. Cover and chill until ready to serve.

4 | *Avocado and Seafood Salad*

Preparation time
20 minutes

Serves 4

Calories
162 per portion

You will need
2 cooked scallops, cut into thin strips
12 cooked mussels, shelled
50 g / 2 oz shelled cooked prawns
2 tablespoons mayonnaise
1½ tablespoons lemon juice
½ tablespoon dry sherry
1 teaspoon tomato purée
Tabasco sauce
2 avocados
shredded lettuce
lemon slices to garnish

Mix together the scallops, mussels, prawns, mayonnaise, ½ teaspoon lemon juice, sherry, tomato purée and Tabasco sauce to taste. Cover and chill until ready to serve.

Halve, stone and peel the avocados, then brush with the remaining lemon juice.

Arrange the lettuce on individual plates. Top with the avocado halves, then divide the filling equally between the avocados. Serve at once, garnished with lemon.

Cook's Tip

If mango isn't available, another suitable exotic fruit is papaya, also known as paw-paw. Halve the fruit, scoop out and discard the seeds, then peel and dice the flesh.

Cook's Tip

For a festive finish, top each salad with bright red lumpfish roe. Crab meat, poached salmon and smoked salmon can all be added to this filling.

5 | Guacamole Salad

Preparation time
10 minutes

Serves 4

Calories
155 per portion

You will need
4 tomatoes
2 tablespoons lemon juice
1 tablespoon grated onion
1 teaspoon chopped fresh
   coriander or ½ teaspoon ground
   coriander
¼ teaspoon Tabasco sauce
2 avocados
1 lettuce
fresh coriander sprigs to garnish
25 g / 1 oz packet taco chips to
   serve

Cut the tomatoes into small dice about 5 mm / ¼ inch square and place in a bowl. Add the lemon juice, onion, coriander and Tabasco sauce and mix well.

Halve, stone and peel the avocados, then cut the flesh into dice the same size as the tomatoes; add to the bowl. Beat with a wooden spoon until the avocado has thickened the juices, but there are still cubes of avocado and tomato visible.

Arrange the lettuce leaves on four individual plates. Spoon the guacamole on top of the lettuce and garnish with coriander sprigs. Serve with taco chips or crisps, for dipping.

6 | Avocado and Bean Pâté

Preparation time
5 minutes

Serves 4

Calories
167 per portion

You will need
1 small garlic clove, peeled and
   halved
1 avocado, peeled and stoned
½ × 400-g / 14-oz can haricot
   beans, drained and rinsed
½ teaspoon mild curry powder
1 teaspoon tomato purée
1 tablespoon milk
2 teaspoons lemon juice

For the garnish
tomato wedges
haricot beans
parsley sprigs

Rub the inside of a bowl with the cut sides of the garlic. Mash the avocado flesh and place in the bowl. Mash the beans and add to the avocado, then stir in the curry powder, tomato purée, milk and lemon juice, beating to form a smooth paste.

Serve at once, with wholemeal melba toast, garnished with tomato wedges, beans and a parsley sprig.

Cook's Tip

Prepare just before serving or else the avocado flesh will turn an unappetizing grey colour. For a spicier version, stir in a crushed, dried red pepper.

Cook's Tip

To make your own melba toast, cut very thin slices from an unsliced loaf or French stick using a long, serrated knife. Place in a 150C / 300 F / Gas 2 oven until dry and the edges turn up. Store in an airtight tin.

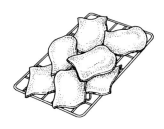

7 | *Spinach and Sardine Pâté*

Preparation time
15 minutes, plus
cooling and setting

Cooking time
10 minutes

Serves 6-8

Calories
225 per portion

You will need
500 g / 1¼ lb spinach, stalks
    removed and washed
salt
15 g / ½ oz powdered gelatine
1 chicken stock cube
300 ml / ½ pint boiling water
1 × 100 g / 4 oz can sardines in oil
2 eggs, hard-boiled, shelled and
    chopped
150 ml / 5 fl oz soured cream
pepper

Place the spinach in a large saucepan with any water that clings to the leaves and a little salt. Cover and cook for 5-10 minutes, stirring occasionally, until the spinach wilts and is tender. Drain, chop roughly and place in a mixing bowl.

Dissolve the gelatine and stock cube in the water. Stir into the chopped spinach and leave until cool but not set.

Roughly chop the sardines in their oil and add with the hard-boiled egg to the spinach mixture. Stir in the soured cream and add salt and pepper to taste. Pour into a 1.2 litre / 2 pint soufflé dish or mould. Cover and refrigerate until set.

To serve, either turn out or spoon on to a serving plate. Slice and serve on individual plates.

8 | *Potted Bacon*

Preparation time
20 minutes, plus
chilling

Serves 4

Calories
305 per portion

You will need
275 g / 10 oz lean cooked bacon,
    such as hock or collar, rinded
100 g / 4 oz unsalted butter,
    melted and cooled
4 tablespoons double cream
1 tablespoon chopped fresh
    parsley
1 teaspoon English mustard
2 tablespoons dry sherry
pinch ground nutmeg
1 red pepper, cored, seeded and
    cut into strips

Mince the bacon to coarse or fine consistency, as you like. Stir three-quarters of the butter into the bacon and mix well. Stir in the cream, parsley, mustard and sherry, and add nutmeg and pepper, to taste.

Turn the mixture into a serving dish and pack it down firmly, using the back of a spoon.

Pour on the remaining butter (it may be necessary to melt it again) and tip the dish to spread the butter in a thin film. Cover the dish with foil or cling film and chill for at least 1 hour.

Meanwhile, cut the pepper strips into small diamond or leaf shapes to garnish the top of the dish. Serve chilled with hot buttered toast.

Cook's Tip

This easy-to-make pâté is also attractively presented when prepared in individual ramekins. Spoon the mixture into 100 g / 4 oz ramekins, cover with cling film and chill until ready to serve. Individual moulds, as well as a large **single one, can be prepared a day in advance.**

Cook's Tip

This prepared recipe will keep for up to four days, covered, in the refrigerator. The pepper strips for the garnish can also be prepared a day ahead.

9 | Duchy of Cornwall Pâté

Preparation time
25 minutes

Serves 8

Calories
353 per portion

You will need
1 garlic clove, peeled and crushed
175 g /6 oz skinned smoked cod's
    roe
pepper
2 tablespoons chopped parsley
150 ml / ¼ pint oil
2 tablespoons lemon juice
2 tablespoons boiling water
1 smoked mackerel fillet, about
    225 g /8 oz, skinned and flaked
8 large flat mushrooms
50 g / 2 oz butter
1 tablespoon oil
8 slices bread, cut into rounds
parsley sprigs to garnish

Combine the garlic, roe, pepper to taste and parsley in a liquidizer or food processor and blend until smooth. Gradually add half the oil, then add the lemon juice and water. Add the remaining oil and blend. Beat in the smoked mackerel, then cover and chill.

Remove the mushroom stalks and reserve. Melt the butter and oil and lightly fry the mushroom caps and stalks. Remove the mushrooms from the pan with a slotted spoon. Drain well. Fry the bread in the remaining fat until golden on both sides, then drain well.

To serve, spoon some of the pâté into each mushroom cap and top with the chopped stalks. Place on top of the bread rounds on individual plates. Serve garnished with parsley sprigs.

Cook's Tip

If large, flat mushrooms aren't available, serve this creamy paté on its own with wholemeal toast or strips of pitta bread.

10 | Liver and Mushroom Pâté

Preparation time
8 minutes

Cooking time
8 minutes

Serves 4–6

Calories
142 per portion

You will need
225 g / 8 oz chicken livers, thawed
    if frozen and trimmed
25 g / 1 oz butter or margarine
1 onion, peeled and finely
    chopped
2 garlic cloves, peeled and
    crushed
50 g / 2 oz mushrooms, wiped
    and sliced
1 teaspoon dried mixed herbs
2 teaspoons brandy or sherry
2 teaspoons soy sauce
½ teaspoon tomato purée
pepper
watercress sprigs and lemon
    slices to garnish

Cut the livers into small pieces.

Melt the butter or margarine and fry the onion for 2 minutes, stirring. Stir in the garlic, livers and mushrooms and stir-fry for 4–5 minutes until the chicken livers start to crumble.

Set aside to cool a little, then transfer to a liquidizer or food processor with the herbs, brandy or sherry, soy sauce, tomato purée and pepper to taste. Blend until smooth. Cover and chill until ready to serve.

Serve with fingers of hot wholemeal toast, garnished with watercress and lemon slices.

Cook's Tip

For a coarser pâté, you can mash all the ingredients together with a potato masher. If you do this, make sure the onion and garlic are very finely chopped and crushed.

11 | *Smoked Trout Pâté*

Preparation time
*20 minutes, plus
chilling*

Serves 4–6

Calories
210 per portion

You will need
*75 g / 3 oz butter or margarine,
    softened
2 smoked trout, skinned and
    flaked
1 teaspoon finely grated lemon
    rind
150 ml / ¼ pint single cream
1 tablespoon horseradish sauce
1 teaspoon chopped fresh dill, or
    ½ teaspoon dried
1 teaspoon chopped fresh parsley
1–2 tablespoons lemon juice
pepper or cayenne pepper
lemon slices to garnish*

Cream the butter until it is soft, then beat in the fish. Gradually incorporate the remaining ingredients until the pâté is smooth and light.

Alternatively, place all the ingredients in a liquidizer or food processor and work until smooth.

Spoon into individual pots or one large bowl. Cover with cling film and chill until ready to serve. Serve with lemon slices.

12 | *Smoked Mackerel and Cream Cheese Pâté*

Preparation time
20 minutes

Serves 4

Calories
607 per portion

You will need
*350 g / 12 oz smoked mackerel
    fillets, skinned and flaked
75 g / 3 oz butter, softened
175 g / 6 oz full fat soft cheese
2 teaspoons lemon juice
1 tablespoon chopped fresh
    chives
pepper
4 small bay leaves to garnish*

Cream together the butter and cheese, then stir in the fish, lemon juice, chives and pepper to taste. Beat until the mixture is smooth.

Divide the pâté between four individual ramekin dishes. Place a bay leaf in each dish to garnish. Serve with wholemeal toast if liked.

Cook's Tip

When time is short, this pâté can be served at room temperature as soon as it is made. If you don't have any dill, increase the amount of parsley or use finely chopped chives or spring onion tops.

Cook's Tip

Another attractive way to present this pâté is with a layer of melted butter poured over the top of each portion. Press a bay leaf into each before the butter sets. Cool, then cover with cling film. Refrigerate for up to two days.

13 | *Smoked Trout and Orange Salad*

Preparation time
20 minutes, plus chilling

Serves 4
as a light main course

Calories
206 per portion

You will need
350 g / 12 oz smoked trout fillets, skinned and boned
½ cucumber, very thinly sliced
3 oranges, peeled and segmented
3 sticks celery, thinly sliced

For the garnish
lettuce leaves
1 bunch watercress
cayenne pepper

For the dressing
40 g / 1½ oz sweet apple, grated
1 tablespoon lemon juice
3 tablespoons mayonnaise
1½ teaspoons creamed horseradish

To make the dressing, mix the apple with the lemon juice, mayonnaise and creamed horseradish, blending well.

Flake the smoked trout into bite-sized pieces. Place in a bowl with the cucumber, orange segments and celery, tossing gently to mix.

To serve, line a serving dish with a few lettuce leaves. Top with the smoked trout salad and spoon over the dressing. Chill lightly before serving. Garnish with sprigs of watercress and sprinkle with cayenne pepper.

14 | *Mussel Salad*

Preparation time
40 minutes

Cooking time
10 minutes

Serves 6

Calories
119 per portion

You will need
2 litres / 3½ pints fresh mussels, well scrubbed
2 tablepoons oil
2 shallots or 1 small onion, peeled and thinly chopped
4 tablespoons dry white wine
salt and pepper
1 lettuce, shredded, to serve
2 tablespoons olive oil
1 tablespoon lemon juice
2 tablespoons chopped fresh parsley

Discard any mussels that have broken shells or that do not close when tapped.

Heat the oil in a large saucepan and gently fry the shallots or onion for 5 minutes until lightly browned.

Pour in the wine and add a little salt and pepper. Add the mussels. Cover the pan, bring to the boil and cook for 5 minutes, shaking the pan occasionally, until all the mussels have opened. Discard any that do not open.

Remove the mussels, reserving the liquid, and take them out of their shells. Boil the liquid to reduce to 150 ml / ¼ pint, strain and leave to cool.

Arrange the shredded lettuce over the base of a serving dish or individual plates. Place the mussels on top. Mix the cooking liquid with the olive oil, lemon juice and parsley and pour over the mussels.

Cook's Tip

Lightly toasted almond flakes can be sprinkled over the top of this salad. They add extra flavour and texture as well as making an attractive garnish.

Cook's Tip

If fresh mussels are not available, use 350 g / 12 oz canned or frozen shelled mussels. Toss them in 150 ml / ¼ pint French dressing with 1 tablespoon lemon juice. Sprinkle with chopped fresh parsley.

15 | *Seafood Salad*

Preparation time
20 minutes

Serves 4

Calories
141 per portion

You will need
*1 small red pepper, cored, seeded
    and thinly sliced
2 carrots, peeled and cut into
    matchstick strips
2 sticks of celery, cut into
    matchstick strips
a few lettuce leaves
2 small onions, peeled and thinly
    sliced
225 g / 8 oz peeled cooked
    prawns
1 × 200-g / 7-oz can tuna, drained
8 stuffed olives, sliced*

For the dressing
*6 tablespoons olive oil
2 tablespoons lemon juice
2 garlic cloves, peeled and
    crushed
2 teaspoons fresh marjoram,
    chopped, or 1 teaspoon dried
salt and pepper*

Mix the pepper, carrot, celery and onion together. Make a bed of lettuce leaves on four small dishes or plates. Top with the mixed vegetables.

Mix together the prawns, tuna and olives and arrange on the salad.

To make the dressing, place all the ingredients in a jar and shake well to mix. Pour the dressing over the salad to serve.

Cook's Tip

To save time when serving, prepare the salad up to 8 hours in advance and keep chilled, covered with cling film. The dressing will keep for several days, covered, in the refrigerator.

16 | *Seafood Stuffed Lettuce*

Preparation time
15 minutes

Serves 4

Calories
470 per portion

You will need
*1 large, round lettuce
4 hard-boiled eggs, shelled and
    chopped
225 g / 8 oz shelled cooked
    prawns
175 g / 6 oz crab meat, fresh,
    frozen or canned
150 ml / ¼ pint Anchovy
    mayonnaise (below)
1 tablespoon lemon juice
2 tablespoons chopped fresh
    chives
2 tablespoons chopped fresh
    parsley
salt and pepper
8 unshelled cooked prawns to
    garnish*

Remove and discard the ragged outside leaves from the lettuce, but keep the rest whole. Carefully wash and shake to remove excess water. Leave to drain upside down on paper towels or a clean tea towel.

To make the stuffing, place the eggs in a bowl and add the prawns and crab meat. Stir in the Anchovy mayonnaise, lemon juice, chives and parsley. Add salt and pepper to taste.

Place the lettuce on a plate. Gently pull apart the leaves to make a hole in the centre. Pluck out the lettuce heart.

Spoon the stuffing into the centre of the lettuce. Garnish with unshelled prawns if liked.

Cook's Tip

To make the Anchovy mayonnaise, add 1 × 50-g / 2-oz can anchovy fillets with the oil and 1 tablespoon tomato purée to 300–450 g / ½–¾ pint mayonnaise and beat until well blended. Store, covered, in the refrigerator.

17 | Smoked Salmon and Tarama Timbales

Preparation time	**You will need**
15 minutes, plus chilling	oil for greasing
	175 g / 6 oz smoked salmon, thinly sliced
Makes 4	175 g / 6 oz taramasalata
	175 g / 6 oz full fat soft cheese
Calories	dash Tabasco sauce
484 per portion	juice of ½ lemon
	pinch cayenne pepper
	4 lemon twists to garnish

Lightly grease four ramekins. Line the dishes with smoked salmon, trimming to fit. Chop any remaining pieces of smoked salmon.

Mix together the taramasalata, soft cheese, Tabasco sauce, lemon juice and cayenne pepper. Add any remaining salmon.

Divide the mixture between the four dishes. Level the tops, cover with cling film and chill for 2–3 hours.

Carefully turn out of the ramekins on to individual dishes. Garnish with twists of lemon and serve.

18 | Monkfish Aurore

Preparation time	**You will need**
20 minutes, plus cooling	450 g / 1 lb monkfish, skinned
	150 ml / ¼ pint mayonnaise
	3 tablespoons double or whipping cream, whipped
Cooking time	1 tablespoon lemon juice
10 minutes	1 teaspoon tomato purée
	1 tablespoon chopped capers
Serves 4	1 tablespoon chopped gherkins
	salt and pepper
Calories	
380 per portion	**For the garnish**
	4 gherkin fans
	4 lemon slices

Cut the monkfish into 2.5 cm / 1 inch cubes. Put into a pan of lightly salted water and bring to the boil, then simmer for 10 minutes until cooked through. Remove from the heat and leave to cool in the liquid.

Mix together the mayonnaise, cream, lemon juice, tomato purée, capers, gherkins and salt and pepper to taste.

Strain the fish and add to the mayonnaise mixture. Divide between four plates. Garnish with gherkins and lemon slices.

Cook's Tip

Taramasalata is a creamy, soft pâté made from cod's roe. It is pale pink, and available from supermarkets and delicatessens. If you have any left over, serve it as a dip with strips of pitta bread or vegetable sticks.

Cook's Tip

A firm fish with a rich flavour, monkfish was once known as the 'poor man's lobster'. Today, however, because of its popularity, the price has greatly increased. Cod is a less expensive fish equally suitable for this recipe.

19 | *Scallop Ceviche with Herbs*

Preparation time
20 minutes, plus
marinating

Serves 4

Calories
179 per portion

You will need
10 large scallops
150 ml / ¼ pint lemon juice
1½ tablespoons chopped shallot
½ tablespoon finely chopped fresh
  tarragon
½ tablespoon finely chopped fresh
  dill
½ tablespoon finely chopped fresh
  chives
½ tablespoon finely chopped fresh
  parsley
1½ tablespoons sunflower oil
parsley sprigs to garnish

Detach the scallops from their shells and scrape off the beard-like fringe and intestinal thread. Cut away the orange coral. Wash the white parts and pat dry. Cut in slices about 5 mm / ¼ inch thick. Wash and prepare the coral in the same way, if you like.

Reserve 4 medium shells, scrub them well and leave to drain. Place the sliced scallops in a bowl and pour over the lemon juice to cover them. Cover with cling film and refrigerate for 24 hours, stirring occasionally.

When ready to serve, drain the lemon juice from the scallops and stir in the oil. Add the shallots and herbs and mix well. Spoon on to the shells and serve immediately, garnished with parsley sprigs, and with brown bread and butter.

20 | *Papaya Prawns*

Preparation time
20 minutes, plus
chilling

Serves 8

Calories
209 per portion

You will need
4 large papayas, about 225 g /
  8 oz each
2 teaspoons fresh lime juice
8 large cooked king prawns,
  peeled and chopped
1 red pepper, cored, seeded and
  chopped
120 ml / 4 fl oz mayonnaise
2 teaspoons freshly grated
  horseradish
finely grated rind of 1 lime

For the garnish
lime twists
few whole unpeeled cooked
  prawns (optional)

Halve the papayas lengthways, scoop out and discard the seeds. Cut the flesh into small dice, leaving the shells intact.

Mix the papaya flesh with the lime juice, prawns, red pepper, mayonnaise, horseradish and grated lime rind, blending well.

Spoon the papaya and prawn mixture back into the reserved shells. Place one shell on individual serving plates.

Chill lightly before serving. Garnish with twists of lime and a few unpeeled prawns if liked. Serve with triangles of brown bread and butter.

Cook's Tip

Marinating the scallops in the lemon juice has the effect of 'cooking' the fish. This method of preparing fish is especially popular in Mediterranean countries.

Cook's Tip

A papaya is ready to eat when its skin has turned yellow and it feels tender if slightly pressed. This dish is also good when avocados are used instead of the papaya.

21 | *King Prawn Fritters with Green Sauce*

Preparation time
20 minutes

Cooking time
5 minutes

Serves 4

Calories
528 per portion

You will need
8 king prawns, peeled
1 tablespoon lemon juice
salt and pepper
50 g / 2 oz plain flour
2 tablespoons olive oil
4 tablespoons water
1 egg white

For the sauce
150 ml / ¼ pint mayonnaise
3 tablespoons chopped parsley
2 teaspoons chopped fresh basil
1 tablespoon pine nuts, chopped
1 tablespoon pistachio nuts, chopped
1 garlic clove, peeled and crushed

Place the prawns in a bowl and sprinkle over lemon juice and salt and pepper.

Mix together all the sauce ingredients until thoroughly blended. Cover and chill until ready to serve.

To make the batter, place the flour in a bowl with salt and pepper. Add the olive oil and water and mix to form a smooth batter. Whisk the egg white until it forms soft peaks. Fold into the batter.

Heat the oil to 180–190C / 350–375F or until a cube of bread browns in 30 seconds. Dip the prawns in the batter and deep-fry for 5 minutes until golden.

Drain well on paper towels. Garnish with cucumber slices and serve with the sauce.

22 | *Trout Goujons with Hazelnuts*

Preparation time
15 minutes, plus chilling

Cooking time
10 minutes

Serves 4

Calories
283 per portion

You will need
2 trout, skinned and filleted
50 g / 2 oz hazelnuts without their skins, chopped
100 g / 4 oz fresh white breadcrumbs
25 g / 1 oz seasoned plain flour
2 eggs, beaten
oil for deep frying
1 grapefruit, skinned and segmented

Cut the trout into strips diagonally.

Mix the hazelnuts and breadcrumbs in a bowl. Put the flour on a plate and put the eggs in another bowl.

Coat the fish with the flour, then dip into the egg and roll in the breadcrumb mixture. Chill for 30 minutes.

Heat the oil to 180–190C / 350–375F or until a cube of bread browns in 30 seconds. Deep-fry the fish for 5 minutes until golden and cooked through. Fry in batches.

Drain well on kitchen paper, keeping hot while other batches are cooking. Divide between four plates and serve with the grapefruit segments.

Cook's Tip

Folding a whisked egg white into the batter helps make it light and crispy. Use the batter as soon as the egg white has been added.

Cook's Tip

It is important to test that the oil is the correct temperature before frying. If it is too hot, the coating will burn before the fish cooks through; if it is too cool the goujons will not be crisp nor will they cook through.

23 | Grilled Fish Cakes

Preparation time
7 minutes

Cooking time
8–10 minutes

Serves 4–6

Calories
265 per portion

You will need
1 × 200-g / 7-oz can pink salmon, drained and flaked
450 g / 1 lb potatoes, peeled and boiled
25 g / 1 oz butter or margarine
1 tablespoon milk (optional)
1 tablespoon chopped fresh parsley
pepper
finely grated rind of ½ lemon
1 tablespoon plain flour
1 tablespoon oil
parsley sprigs to garnish

Mash the salmon in a bowl, including the bones and skin.

Mash the potatoes with the butter, then add the milk if the mixture seems too dry. Add the salmon, parsley, pepper to taste and lemon rind and mix well. With lightly floured hands, shape into flat, round cakes about 1 cm / ½ inch thick.

Brush the grill pan with oil and arrange the cakes on the base. Dab the tops of the fish cakes with a little more oil. Cook under a preheated moderate grill for 4–5 minutes, then turn over and cook on the other side for 4–5 minutes until golden.

Serve at once, garnished with parsley.

24 | Tomato and Tuna Redskins

Preparation time
20 minutes

Cooking time
30 minutes

Oven temperature
180C, 350F, Gas 4

Serves 4

Calories
251 per portion

You will need
4 large beefsteak tomatoes
25 g / 1 oz butter
1 onion, peeled and chopped
1 × 200-g / 7-oz can tuna fish in oil, drained and flaked
75 g / 3 oz fresh white breadcrumbs
1 tablespoon chopped fresh parsley
1 egg, beaten
salt and pepper
1 × 50-g / 2-oz can anchovy fillets in oil

For the garnish
small black olives
parsley sprigs

Slice the tops off the tomatoes. Scoop out the insides of the tomatoes and discard the inner seeds.

Melt the butter and fry the onion for 5 minutes. Remove from the heat and stir in the tuna, breadcrumbs, parsley, egg and salt and pepper to taste. Spoon the mixture into the prepared tomatoes.

Drain the anchovies, reserving the oil, and arrange over the top of the tomatoes. Place in an ovenproof dish and drizzle with the anchovy oil.

Cook in a preheated oven for 20 minutes or until tender. Garnish with black olives and parsley and serve hot with crusty bread.

Cook's Tip

Crab meat or tuna work as well in this recipe. If you use crab meat, pick through it to remove any pieces of shell or bone. Look for fish packed in brine rather than oil for a substantially lower fat content.

Cook's Tip

This dish will probably need very little added salt. The anchovy fillets are very salty, so only add a little salt, if any, to the breadcrumb mixture.

25 | *Puff Pastry with Leeks*

Preparation time
15 minutes

Cooking time
20 minutes

Oven temperature
220C, 425F, Gas 7

Serves 4

Calories
748 per portion

You will need
1 × 375-g /13-oz packet frozen
    puff pastry, thawed
1 egg, beaten
parsley sprigs to garnish

For the filling
50 g / 2 oz butter
350 g / 12 oz white part of leeks,
    thinly sliced and well washed
juice of ½ lemon
salt and pepper
150 ml / ¼ pint double cream

Roll out the pastry to a rectangle 26 × 150 cm / 10 × 6 inches. Cut into four pieces, each 13 × 7 ½ / 5 × 3 inches.

Score each piece lightly in a diamond pattern and brush the tops with the beaten egg. Place on a moistened baking sheet and bake in a preheated oven for 20 minutes until puffed and golden on top.

Meanwhile, prepare the filling. Melt the butter and cook the leeks for 10 minutes until soft but not browned. Add the lemon juice and salt and pepper to taste and stir well. Add the cream, bring to the boil, stirring constantly and cook for 2–3 minutes until lightly thickened.

When the pastry slices are cooked, remove from the oven and cut each one in half horizontally. Divide the leek mixture between the bottom halves of the pastry slices, then replace the pastry top. Garnish with parsley sprigs and serve at once.

Cook's Tip

Don't be tempted to use single cream to make the creamy leek filling or it may curdle when boiled.

26 | *Leek Terrine with Walnuts and Feta*

Preparation time
25 minutes, plus
chilling

Cooking time
10 minutes

Serves 6

Calories
264 per portion

You will need
20 small young leeks, roots and
    most of green parts trimmed
radicchio or other chicory leaves
75 g / 3 oz Feta cheese, crumbled
50 g / 2 oz walnut halves,
    chopped
salt and pepper

For the dressing
4 tablespoons olive oil
2 tablespoons walnut oil
2 tablespoons wine vinegar
2 tablespoons English mustard

Split the leeks horizontally to within 5 cm / 2 inches of the root end. Wash well. Boil the leeks in salted water for 10 minutes or until tender.

Layer a 450 g / 1 lb loaf tin with the leeks laid head to tail alternately, sprinking each layer with salt and pepper to taste. Place another tin inside the first, pressing down the leeks. Invert both tins so the liquid drains out. Chill for at least 4 hours with a 1 kg / 2 lb weight on top.

Meanwhile, to make the dressing, mix together all the ingredients and season with salt and pepper to taste. Set aside until needed.

Carefully turn out the leek terrine. Using a very sharp knife, cut into 6 thick slices. Place each slice on a plate and surround with the salad leaves. Scatter the walnuts and Feta cheese on top of the salad. Spoon over some dressing and serve.

Cook's Tip

This is an ideal dish for a dinner party because both the terrine and dressing can be made a day ahead and kept overnight in the refrigerator. Let the terrine come to room temperature before serving.

27 | *Asparagus Mousse*

Preparation time
15 minutes, plus setting

Cooking time
20-25 minutes

Serves 6

Calories
137 per portion

You will need
450 g / 1 lb fresh asparagus, well
    trimmed
salt and pepper
300 ml / ½ pint water or milk
25 g / 1 oz butter or margarine
25 g / 1 oz plain flour
15 g / ½ oz powdered gelatine,
    dissolved in 2 tablespoons hot
    water
150 ml / 5 fl oz soured cream
grated rind of ½ lemon
1 tablespoon lemon juice
1 hard-boiled egg, finely chopped

Cut off the asparagus tips with about 5 cm / 2 inches of stem and simmer in salted water for 3-5 minutes until tender but not limp. Remove with a slotted spoon and cool. Chop the remaining asparagus stems into small pieces and add to the water. Cover and simmer for 12-15 minutes until soft. Drain, reserving the cooking water.

Make up the cooking water to 300 ml / ½ pint with water or milk. Melt the butter or margarine and stir in the flour. When smooth, gradually stir in the cooking liquid and bring to the boil, stirring until thickened. Add the asparagus stems and simmer for 3 minutes, stirring occasionally. Pour the sauce into a bowl. Stir in the gelatine and leave until cool but not set. Stir in the soured cream, lemon rind and juice and egg. Add salt and pepper to taste. Pour into a 1.2 litre / 2 pint mould and chill until set. Chill reserved asparagus tips until required.

To serve, turn out of the mould and garnish with reserved asparagus tips.

Cook's Tip

If fresh asparagus is not in season, substitute 450 g / 1 lb frozen asparagus. Simmer the tips for 3 minutes, then the stems for 6-8 minutes. Drain well and proceed with the recipe. This mousse can be made up to one day in advance and chilled. Unmould and garnish just before serving.

28 | *Walnut Pears*

Preparation time
15 minutes

Serves 4

Calories
261 per portion

You will need
2 tablespoons olive oil
2 tablespoons lemon juice
½ teaspoon sugar
salt and pepper
2 large dessert pears
1 small lettuce heart, separated
    into leaves
175 g /6 oz curd cheese
3 tablespoons soured cream
50 g / 2 oz walnut halves,
    chopped

Mix together the oil, lemon juice, sugar and salt and pepper to taste in a bowl.

Halve, core and peel the pears, then toss them in the oil and lemon juice mixture to prevent them turning brown.

Arrange the lettuce leaves on individual plates. Combine the remaining ingredients, adding only half the walnuts. Arrange the pear halves on top, then fill with the cheese mixture and garnish with the reserved walnuts. Serve at once.

Cook's Tip

To peel pears quickly and easily, plunge them in boiling water for just a few seconds. This helps by loosening the skins.

29 | Melon and Parma Ham Salad with Ginger Dressing

Preparation time
10 minutes, plus chilling

Serves 4

Calories
221 per portion

You will need
1 medium honeydew melon, about 1 kg / 2 lb
100 g / 4 oz Parma ham, thinly sliced

For the dressing
25 g / 1 oz stem ginger, finely chopped
2 tablespoons stem ginger syrup
3 tablespoons salad oil
1 teaspoon lemon juice
black pepper

Cut the melon into quarters lengthways. Discard the seeds and cut off the skin. Cut each melon quarter into 4 long slices, making 16 slices altogether.

Cut the Parma ham into long slices about 5 cm / 2 inches wide.

Arrange the melon slices on individual plates, interleaved with slices of ham.

To make the dressing, place the stem ginger in a bowl. Add the ginger syrup, oil, lemon juice and pepper and whisk together.

Spoon the dressing evenly over each serving of melon and ham. Cover and chill for ½ hour before serving.

30 | Summer Melon Salad

Preparation time
15 minutes

Serves 4

Calories
115 per portion

You will need
1 small ripe melon
100 g / 4 oz strawberries, hulled
1 × 7.5 cm / 3 inch piece cucumber
1 small crisp lettuce, shredded
4 tablespoons French dressing
2 tablespoons chopped fresh mint
salt and pepper
15 g / ½ oz flaked almonds to garnish

Cut the melon into quarters, then remove the seeds and skin. Scoop the flesh into balls or cut into cubes.

Cut the strawberries and cucumber into thin slices.

To serve, arrange the shredded lettuce on individual plates or a large serving dish. Arrange the pieces of melon, strawberry and cucumber on top of the lettuce.

Mix the French dressing with the mint and add salt and pepper to taste. Pour over the salad just before serving and sprinkle with the almonds. This goes very well with a selection of hard and soft cheeses, or ham.

Cook's Tip

This flavourful starter is based on the popular Italian ham, also called prosciutto, a speciality of Parma in northern Italy. The ham is dry salted for a month, then hung and cured in a large shed for six months. Look for it in Italian food shops or pre-packaged in supermarkets. It is expensive but many shops sell end cuts for a reduced price, which are suitable for this recipe. If you are buying it freshly cut, ask for wafer-thin slices.

Cook's Tip

An attractive way to present this refreshing starter is in a scooped out melon shell. Use small ogen melons, allowing half a melon for each serving. You could cut the melons with a zig zag edge for a more decorative effect.

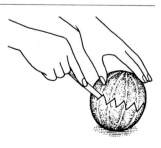

31 | *Melon with Strawberries*

Preparation time
10 minutes, plus chilling

Serves 6

Calories
106 per portion

You will need
350 g / 12 oz hulled strawberries
4 tablespoons kirsch or brandy
  (optional)
2 ripe melons, well chilled
mint sprigs to decorate

Slice the strawberries and place in a bowl. Sprinkle the kirsch or brandy over the strawberries and toss gently. Set aside.

Cut the melons in half and remove the seeds. Scoop out the melon flesh into small balls, using a melon baller or teaspoon.

Add the melon balls to the strawberries and carefully mix the fruits together. Transfer to individual dishes, cover and chill until ready to serve.

To serve, decorate each bowl with mint sprigs.

32 | *Tropical Fruits in Sherry*

Preparation time
10 minutes, plus
marinating

Serves 4

Calories
84 per portion

You will need
1 papaya
2 kiwi fruit
2 small bananas
1 tablespoon lemon juice
150 ml / ¼ pint medium or dry
  sherry
fresh mint sprigs to garnish

Peel the papaya, cut it in half and scrape out the black pips. Cut the flesh into long slices and put into a bowl.

Peel the kiwi fruit, cut into slices and add to the bowl.

Skin the bananas and cut into slices. Put into another bowl and sprinkle with the lemon juice to stop them discolouring.

Add the bananas to the other fruits and pour the sherry over them. Cover and marinate for 2 hours in the refrigerator.

Spoon the fruits carefully into four bowls, adding a little of the sherry to each one. Serve garnished with mint.

Cook's Tip

A delicious combination is to use a Charente melon from France and replace the kirsch with Pineau de Charentes. This is a drink from the same region as the melon, made from undistilled wine and brandy.

Cook's Tip

Lychees and fresh pineapple chunks can be added to the above combination of fruit or used as substitutes. Lychees, originally from China, have a brittle pinkish-brown shell that is peeled away to reveal the sweet white fruit.

Soups and Snacks

A busy cook can never have too many recipes for flavour-filled soups. Hot or cold, smooth or chunky, most soups are versatile enough to be a starter or make a light meal, if partnered with crusty bread and perhaps a salad. Try the quick and easy snacks that follow. No matter how busy you are, there are ideas for light and satisfying meals.

33 | Herby Chicken Soup

Preparation time
5 minutes

Cooking time
10–12 minutes

Serves 4

Calories
112 per portion

You will need
2 teaspoons oil
1 onion, peeled and finely chopped
175 g / 6 oz cooked boneless chicken, skinned and chopped
900 ml / 1½ pints hot chicken stock
1 tablespoon soy sauce
small pinch dried sage
small pinch ground cinnamon
½ small garlic clove, crushed
2 tablespoons skimmed dried milk, mixed with
2 tablespoons cold water
1 tablespoon chopped fresh parsley
pepper

Heat the oil and fry the onion for 3 minutes, stirring, until transparent. Add the chicken, stock, soy sauce, sage, cinnamon and garlic, then bring to the boil, cover and simmer for 5 minutes.

Stir a little of the soup into the milk, then slowly add this mixture to the pan, heating gently while you stir. Add the parsley and pepper to taste.

Serve hot with crusty wholemeal rolls.

34 | Cheese and Potato Soup

Preparation time
10 minutes

Cooking time
20 minutes

Serves 4

Calories
295 per portion

You will need
50 g / 2 oz butter or margarine
3 potatoes, peeled and diced
2 onions, peeled and diced
900 ml / 1½ pints chicken or vegetable stock
1 teaspoon English mustard
150 ml / ¼ pint single cream
100 g / 4 oz Cheddar cheese, grated
salt and pepper
1 tablespoon chopped fresh parsley

Melt the butter and fry the potatoes and onions until golden. Add the stock and bring to the boil, then simmer for 10–15 minutes until the vegetables are tender but the potatoes are still holding their shape.

Add the mustard and cream and heat through for 2–3 minutes without boiling.

Stir in the cheese, then season to taste with salt and pepper.

Serve hot, garnished with parsley.

Cook's Tip

Do not boil the soup after the reconstituted dried milk has been added or it may curdle. Skimmed dried milk is a concentrated source of nutrients, particularly calcium, but with very little fat.

Cook's Tip

To make chicken stock, boil a chicken carcass or bones with onions, celery and carrots. Add fresh parsley, thyme, a bay leaf and black peppercorns. Skim the surface, then slowly simmer for 2–3 hours.

35 | *Pea and Ham Soup*

Preparation time
4 minutes

Cooking time
12–15 minutes

Serves 4

Calories
126 per portion

You will need
1 tablespoon butter or margarine
2 onions, peeled and thinly sliced
450 g / 1 lb peas, shelled
600 ml / 1 pint boiling vegetable
   stock
1 tablespoon soy sauce
salt and pepper
2 slices lean cooked ham, diced

Melt the butter and fry the onions for 4 minutes, stirring, without browning. Add the peas and boiling stock, bring back to the boil, then simmer for 8–10 minutes for fresh peas (5–6 minutes if frozen).

Add a little cold water to cool, then purée in a liquidizer or food processor until smooth, in two batches if necessary. Return to the pan, add the soy sauce, pepper and ham and simmer for 2 minutes, stirring.

Serve hot with wholemeal rolls.

36 | *Watercress Soup*

Preparation time
4 minutes

Cooking time
12 minutes

Serves 4

Calories
65 per portion

You will need
1 tablespoon butter or margarine
2 onions, peeled and thinly sliced
2 bunches watercress
1 potato, peeled and roughly
   grated
600 ml / 1 pint hot vegetable or
   chicken stock
300 ml / ½ pint cold vegetable or
   chicken stock
1 tablespoon soy sauce
watercress sprigs to garnish

Melt the margarine and fry the onions for 3 minutes, stirring. Add the watercress, potato and hot stock and bring to the boil, then simmer for 6–7 minutes.

Add the cold stock to cool, then purée in a liquidizer or food processor until smooth, in two batches if necessary. Return to the pan, add the soy sauce and reheat gently, stirring.

Serve hot, garnished with watercress and with buttered fingers of wholemeal toast.

Cook's Tip

If fresh peas are out of season, you can use frozen. Add the frozen peas directly to the soup. There isn't any need to thaw them first.

Cook's Tip

To have homemade stock on hand for soup-making, make up large amounts of stock then reduce and freeze in ice cube trays. The flavour of each cube is very concentrated, and they take up less space than pots of stock.

37 | *Minestrone*

Preparation time
8 minutes

Cooking time
20 minutes

Serves 4

Calories
277 per portion

You will need
1 tablespoon butter or margarine
2 onions, peeled and thinly sliced
2 garlic cloves, peeled and
   crushed
900ml / 1½ pints boiling vegetable
   stock
1 tablespoon soy sauce
1 tablespoon tomato purée
1 carrot, roughly grated
100 g / 4 oz mushrooms, wiped
   and sliced
1 celery stick, chopped
1 x 400-g / 14-oz can chick peas or
   haricot beans, drained and
   rinsed
1–2 tablespoons chopped fresh
   parsley
75 g / 3 oz green cabbage,
   shredded
75 g / 3 oz fresh wholemeal
   tagliatelle, cut into short lengths
grated Parmesan cheese to serve

Melt the butter and fry the onions for 4 minutes, stirring. Stir in the garlic, then add the remaining ingredients, except the pasta. Bring to the boil, cover and simmer for 10 minutes.

Add the pasta and bring back to the boil, then simmer, uncovered, for 3 minutes.

Serve hot with a sprinkling of Parmesan cheese.

38 | *Hearty Vegetable Soup*

Preparation time
8 minutes

Cooking time
15–20 minutes

Serves 4

Calories
190 per portion

You will need
1 tablespoon oil
2 onions, peeled and thinly sliced
2 carrots, finely diced
2 small turnips, finely diced
2 celery sticks, finely chopped
2 garlic cloves, peeled and
   crushed
3 potatoes, peeled and cut into
   small sticks
1 tablespoon soy sauce
pepper
1 × 400-g / 14-oz can chopped
   tomatoes
1 × 400-g / 14-oz can haricot
   beans, drained and rinsed
2 heaped tablespoons frozen peas
1 tablespoon chopped fresh
   parsley
boiling water

Heat the oil and fry the onions for 3 minutes, stirring. Add the carrots, turnips, and celery and stir-fry for another minute.

Add the remaining ingredients with enough boiling water just to cover the vegetables. Bring to the boil, then simmer for 10–15 minutes, stirring occasionally.

Serve hot with wholemeal rolls.

Cook's Tip

Dried chick peas or haricot beans can be used instead of the canned variety. Both need overnight soaking in water to cover. Drain, cover with fresh water and boil for 10 minutes. Chick peas then need about 1¼ hours simmering and haricot beans need 40–50 minutes simmering. Skim the surface as necessary, and do not add any salt while cooking as it toughens beans. Although time-consuming, cooking dried beans is much more economical.

Cook's Tip

Dice the carrots and turnips to a uniform size. This way they will both be cooked at the same time without one becoming too mushy.

39 | Mussel and Basil Soup

Preparation time
5 minutes

Cooking time
40–45 minutes

Serves 6

Calories
205 per portion

You will need
4 tablespoons oil
4 onions, peeled and diced
1 small heart celery, diced
1.8 litres / 3 pints water
50 g / 2 oz long-grain rice
750 g / 1½lb tomatoes, skinned, seeded and diced
about 25 small fresh basil leaves
salt
cayenne pepper
1.8 litres / 3 pints mussels, well scrubbed

Heat half the oil and fry the onions for 5 minutes until golden. Add half the celery and cook for 1 minute, then pour on all but 150 ml / ¼ pint water. Bring to the boil, then stir in the rice and cook for 5 minutes.

Add the tomatoes and basil and lightly season with salt and cayenne papper. Cover and cook for 10 minutes or until the rice is tender, then remove from the heat.

Meanwhile, cook the mussels. Discard any mussels that are open. Heat the remaining oil in another large saucepan, add the remaining onions and celery and cook for 10 minutes. Pour in the remaining water, add the mussels and heat for 10 minutes until all the mussels are open. Discard any that remain closed.

Remove the mussels from their shells. Add the mussels and contents of second pan to the rice mixture. Heat through and season to taste. Serve at once.

40 | Chunky Fish Soup

Preparation time
8–10 minutes

Cooking time
15–20 minutes

Serves 4

Calories
143 per portion

You will need
1 tablespoon oil
2 onions, peeled and thinly sliced
1 celery stick, finely chopped
2 garlic cloves, peeled and crushed
1 × 400-g / 14-oz can chopped tomatoes
1 × 175 g / 6 oz portion each of haddock and cod, cut into small pieces
1–2 heaped tablespoons peeled cooked prawns
juice of ½ lemon
½ teaspoon sugar
1 tablespoon chopped fresh parsley
3 pinches ground bay leaves
pinch dried thyme
good pinch powdered saffron
pepper
600 ml / 1 pint hot fish stock

Heat the oil and fry the onions for 2 minutes, without browning. Add the celery and fry for 2 minutes, stirring.

Stir in the remaining ingredients, then bring to the boil, cover and simmer for 8–10 minutes.

Serve hot, with hunks of wholemeal or French bread, crisped in the oven.

Cook's Tip

Long-grain brown rice can be used in this recipe but it will require an extra 5–10 minutes cooking. The soup can be prepared a day ahead and refrigerated overnight. Reheat thoroughly before serving.

Cook's Tip

Homemade fish stock shouldn't be kept in the refrigerator for more than two days. It can, however, be frozen for up to six months.

41 | Prawn Chowder

Preparation time
10 minutes

Cooking time
8–10 minutes

Serves 4

Calories
257 per portion

You will need
50 g / 2 oz butter
2 rashers streaky bacon, rinded
1 onion, peeled and finely
    chopped
900 ml / 1½ pints fish stock
2 large potatoes, peeled and diced
450 g /l lb cooked prawns, peeled
140 ml / ¼ pint single cream
salt and pepper
2 tablespoons chopped fresh
    fennel leaves or parsley

Melt the butter and fry the bacon and onion for 2–3 minutes.

Pour on the fish stock and bring to the boil. Add the potatoes and cook for 4–5 minutes until tender but still holding their shape. Stir in the prawns, cream, salt and pepper to taste and fennel. Heat through but do not boil. Serve at once.

42 | Sweetcorn and Crab Soup

Preparation time
15 minutes

Cooking time
5 minutes

Serves 4

Calories
97 per portion

You will need
1 teaspoon finely chopped root
    ginger
100 g / 4 oz crab meat
2 teaspoons dry sherry
1 egg white
3 teaspoons cornflour
2 tablespoons cold water
600 ml / 1 pint chicken stock
1 teaspoon salt
100 g / 4 oz sweetcorn, drained if
    canned
1 spring onion, finely chopped, to
    garnish

Mix the ginger with the crab and sherry.

Beat the egg white and mix the cornflour to a smooth paste with the water.

Bring the stock to the boil, then add the salt, sweetcorn and crab meat. When it starts to boil again, add the cornflour and water mixture, stirring constantly. Add the egg white, stirring.

Serve hot, garnished with the spring onion.

Cook's Tip

If you buy unshelled prawns, use the shells to make a light fish stock. Simmer the shells with 900 ml / 1½ pints water, 1 bay leaf and 1 sprig fennel or parsley for 10 minutes, skimming the surface as necessary.

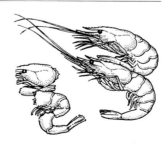

Cook's Tip

To give this soup a more Oriental flavour, substitute sake for the dry sherry. This is a Japanese rice wine which is very potent. You will find it at some Oriental supermarkets and specialist off-licences.

43 | *Cucumber and Yogurt Soup*

Preparation time
10 minutes

Serves 4

Calories
88 per portion

You will need
150 ml / ¼ pint milk
600 ml / 1 pint unsweetened plain yogurt
½ cucumber, peeled and grated
2 tablespoons chopped fresh chives
1 teaspoon chopped fresh mint
1 tablespoon chopped fresh parsley
salt
white pepper

Combine the milk and yogurt in a liquidizer or food processor. Add the remaining ingredients and purée.

Cover and chill until ready to serve. To serve, spoon into well chilled soup bowls and garnish with mint leaves.

44 | *Chilled Melon Soup*

Preparation time
15 minutes, plus chilling

Serves 8

Calories
88 per portion

You will need
2 large Ogen melons, halved and seeds removed
300 ml / ½ pint chicken stock
300 ml / ½ pint unsweetened plain yogurt
150 ml / ¼ pint single cream
salt and pepper

For the croûtons
2 slices bread, crusts removed and diced
oil for frying

Scoop half the melon flesh into balls using a melon baller or teaspoon. Alternatively, dice with a knife.

Place the remaining flesh in a liquidizer or food processor with the stock, yogurt and cream, then purée. Season to taste. Cover and chill until ready to serve.

Meanwhile, heat the oil and fry the bread dice until golden and crisp. Drain well on paper towels.

To serve, ladel into individual bowls and top each with melon balls and croûtons.

Cook's Tip

Several varieties of fresh mint are now widely available. Spearmint and peppermint are two of the strongest. In the summer, when mint is plentiful, freeze finely chopped leaves in ice cube trays so you have a supply.

Cook's Tip

This refreshing summer soup also tastes good with finely chopped fresh mint replacing the croûtons.

45 | *Gazpacho*

Preparation time
25 minutes, plus chilling

Serves 6

Calories
162 per portion

You will need
2 small slices brown bread, crusts removed and torn
600 ml / 1 pint tomato juice
2 garlic cloves, peeled
½ cucumber, peeled and chopped
1 red and 1 green pepper, cored, seeded and chopped
1 large onion, finely chopped
750 g / 1½ lb tomatoes, skinned, seeded and chopped
4 tablespoons olive oil
2 tablespoons red wine vinegar
salt and pepper
¼ teaspoon dried marjoram
¼ teaspoon dried basil
1 tablespoon chopped fresh parsley

For the garnish
croûtons
sliced stuffed green olives
chopped cucumber, peppers and spring onions

Place the bread in a blender with the tomato juice and garlic, leave for 5 minutes, then purée until smooth.

Add the cucumber, peppers, onion, tomatoes, olive oil, vinegar, salt and pepper to taste, marjoram and basil, blending well. Transfer to a chilled soup tureen.

Chill at least 1 hour. Sprinkle with parsley and serve with small bowls of croûtons, olives, cucumber, peppers and onion to garnish. Crusty French bread is a good accompaniment.

Cook's Tip

To make croûtons, fry bread cubes in hot oil for 1 minute until golden and crisp. Drain well on paper towels, then sprinkle with salt. When cool, store in a tight container until ready to use.

46 | *Chilled Provençal Soup*

Preparation time
10 minutes, plus cooling

Cooking time
15 minutes

Serves 4

Calories
188 per portion

You will need
2 tablespoons olive oil
2 garlic cloves, peeled and crushed
2 small aubergines, cubed
450 g / 1 lb tomatoes, skinned and chopped
2 courgettes, sliced
2 tablespoons tomato purée
300 ml / ½ pint water
salt and pepper to taste
grated Parmesan cheese, to serve

For the sauce
2 bunches fresh basil, chopped
4 garlic cloves, peeled
2 tablespoons chopped pine nuts
50 g / 2 oz Parmesan cheese, grated
125 ml / 4 fl oz olive oil

Heat the oil and fry the garlic for 1 minute. Add the aubergines, tomatoes and courgettes. Stir well, reduce the heat and cook, covered, for 5 minutes. Add the tomato purée, water and seasoning. Bring to the boil, then simmer for 5 minutes, until the vegetables are tender.

Meanwhile, to make the sauce, place the basil, garlic, nuts and cheese in a liquidizer and blend until finely ground. Blend in the oil gradually.

Pour the vegetable mixture into the individual bowls and leave to cool. When cold, stir basil sauce into each bowl and sprinkle with Parmesan cheese.

Cook's Tip

Pine nuts are pale oval seeds from the Mediterranean Stone Pine. They are a traditional ingredient in this basil sauce, also known as pesto sauce. Buy pine nuts in small quantities as they do not keep well.

47 | *Curried Egg Sandwiches*

Preparation time
10 minutes

Makes 6

Calories
235 per portion

You will need
6 slices wholemeal bread
25 g / 1 oz butter or margarine, softened
4–6 hard-boiled eggs
1–2 tablespoons milk
¼ teaspoon each mild curry powder and ground coriander
1 small, crisp lettuce
4–6 tablespoons mango or other fruit chutney
3 tomatoes, cut into wedges
2 bananas, sliced and tossed in lemon juice
8–12 walnut halves
¼ cucumber, thinly sliced
1 bunch watercress

Spread one side of each slice of bread with the butter. Mash the eggs together with the milk, curry powder and coriander.

Spread each slice of bread with the egg mixture and top with lettuce leaves. Put 1 tablespoon chutney in the centre of each slice and arrange the remaining ingredients on top.

Cook's Tip

Ring the changes of these tasty snacks by using different types of bread. Granary bread will give a nutty flavour as well as an extra crunchy texture.

48 | *Spicy Club Sandwich*

Preparation time
30 minutes

Cooking time
3–5 minutes

Makes 4

Calories
555 per portion

You will need
100 g / 4 oz boned tandoori chicken, diced
4 tablespoons mayonnaise
1 teaspoon mild curry powder
1 tablespoon seedless raisins
4 rashers back bacon, rinded
8 slices brown bread, crusts removed and toasted
4 slices white bread, crusts removed and toasted
50 g / 2 oz butter, softened
4 lettuce leaves
about 16 thin slices cucumber
1 small green pepper, cored, seeded and sliced
2 tomatoes, thinly sliced
1 tablespoon chopped parsley

Mix the tandoori chicken with the mayonnaise, curry powder and raisins, blending well.

Place the bacon under a preheated hot grill and cook until crisp. Drain well on paper towels.

Spread one side of the brown bread and both sides of the white bread with the butter. Spread the chicken mixture equally over four slices of brown bread. Top each with a slice of white bread. Cover with a lettuce leaf, four cucumber slices and slices of green pepper.

Top each sandwich with a final slice of brown bread. Cover with tomato slices and a rasher of bacon. Sprinkle with chopped parsley and serve with a knife and fork.

Cook's Tip

You can make your own curry powder by combining ground cumin, coriander, tumeric and cayenne pepper. Experiment with the proportions to find a 'heat' you enjoy.

49 | *Union Jack Snacks*

Preparation time
25 minutes

Makes 4

Calories
535 per portion

You will need
4 large round soft rolls topped
   with sesame seeds
75 g / 3 oz butter, softened
100 g / 4oz cold roast Scotch beef,
   shredded
4 tablespoons mayonnaise
1–2 teaspoons creamed
   horseradish
1 tablespoon snipped fresh chives
4 lettuce leaves
100 g / 4 oz mature English
   Cheddar cheese, thinly sliced
1 tomato, thinly sliced
2 tablespoons ploughman's or
   chunky brown pickle
1 leek, very thinly sliced and well
   washed
1 teaspoon grated lemon rind
1 tablespoon seedless raisins

Cut three horizontal slits in each roll but do not cut through the bread to the other side. Spread the bread layers with butter.

Mix the beef with half of the mayonnaise, the horseradish and chives, blending well.

Place a lettuce leaf on the bottom layer of each roll and top with an equal quantity of the beef filling. Fill the middle layer of the rolls with slices of cheese, topped with slices of tomato and the pickle.

Mix the leek with the lemon rind, remaining mayonnaise and raisins, blending well, and fill the top layer of the rolls. Press down lightly on each roll before serving.

Cook's Tip

This snack makes the most of leftover Sunday roasts. The Scotch beef can be replaced with lamb. Omit the horseradish and chives and stir 1–2 teaspoons mint sauce into the mayonnaise.

50 | *Grilled Cheese and Asparagus Sandwiches*

Preparation time
5 minutes

Cooking time
4–5 minutes

Makes 4

Calories
263 per portion

You will need
4 slices wholemeal bread
40 g / 1½ oz butter
4 tomatoes, sliced
salt and pepper
12 canned asparagus spears,
   drained
100 g / 4 oz Cheshire cheese,
   grated

Place the slices of bread under a preheated hot grill and toast until golden on one side.

Turn the bread slices over and spread generously with the butter. Top with the tomato slices. Sprinkle with salt and pepper to taste, then add the asparagus spears and cheese.

Place under a preheated moderate grill and cook 4–5 minutes until golden and bubbly. Serve at once.

Cook's Tip

Cheshire cheese is one of the oldest English cheeses. It is either red or white and has a crumbly texture. If you don't have any Cheshire, use grated Cheddar.

51 | *Cheese and Tuna Muffins*

Preparation time
10 minutes

Cooking time
15–20 minutes

Oven temperature
190C, 375F, Gas 5

Makes 8

Calories
233 per portion

You will need
4 wholemeal or cheese muffins, split
1 onion, peeled and sliced into rings
2 × 200-g / 7-oz cans tuna in brine, drained and flaked
50 g / 2 oz alfalfa sprouts
3 tablespoons mayonnaise
3 tablespoons soured cream
3 tablespoons sunflower seeds
salt and pepper
75 g / 3 oz Cheddar cheese, grated
2 tomatoes, thinly sliced

Toast the muffins on their cut sides under a preheated hot grill. Place on a large baking sheet and top each with an equal quantity of the onion.

Mix the tuna with the alfalfa sprouts, mayonnaise, soured cream, sunflower seeds and salt and pepper to taste, blending well. Spread equally over the muffin halves. Sprinkle with the cheese and top each with a slice of tomato.

Cook in a preheated oven for 15–20 minutes until golden, bubbly and heated through. Serve while still hot.

Cook's Tip

To reduce the calories in this tasty snack, use low-fat mayonnaise. Also, Dutch Edam cheese contains fewer calories than Cheddar, a high-fat cheese.

52 | *Salami and Mozzarella Snack Toasts*

Preparation time
15 minutes

Cooking time
10 minutes

Makes 4

Calories
274 per portion

You will need
4 thick slices crusty bread
100 g / 4 oz salami, rinded and thinly sliced
4 tomatoes, skinned and sliced
salt and pepper
1 green or yellow pepper, cored, seeded and sliced
75 g / 3 oz Mozzarella cheese, thinly sliced
1 teaspoon dried mixed herbs
4–8 small black olives
parsley sprigs to garnish

Place the bread under a preheated hot grill and toast until golden on one side.

Turn the bread slices over and cover with the salami and tomatoes, adding salt and pepper to taste.

Top with the pepper slices and cheese. Sprinkle with the herbs, and place under a preheated moderate grill and toast for 10 minutes until cooked through and bubbly. Serve hot, topped with the black olives and garnished with parsley sprigs.

Cook's Tip

Vary the flavour of this Italian-style snack each time you make it by using a different type of salami. Supermarkets stock excellent choices from France as well as Italy.

53 | Mushroom and Beef Stroganoff Toast Toppers

Preparation time
15 minutes

Cooking time
5 minutes

Serves 4

Calories
529 per portion

You will need
450 g / 1 lb rare roast beef
salt and pepper
25 g / 1 oz butter
2 tablespoons finely chopped
    onion
175 g / 6 oz button mushrooms,
    wiped and sliced
5 tablespoons mayonnaise
5 tablespoons soured cream
pinch cayenne pepper
1 tablespoon chopped fresh
    chives
4 slices wholemeal or rye bread
curly endive or watercress sprigs

Slice the beef across the grain into fairly thick slices. Shred into fine strips about 5 cm / 2 inches long. Season generously with salt and pepper to taste.

Melt the butter, then add the onion and cook for 2 minutes. Add the mushrooms and cook for a further 2 minutes. Remove from the heat and stir in the mayonnaise, cream, cayenne pepper and chives.

Place the slices of bread under a preheated hot grill and toast until golden on both sides.

Add the beef to the stroganoff mixture and heat for 1 minute over a very gentle heat. Do not boil. Top the slices of toast with curly endive or watercress and spoon over the stroganoff. Serve at once.

Cook's Tip

To lower the overall fat content of these snacks, replace the soured cream with Greek yogurt. Do not boil after the yogurt is added or it may curdle.

54 | Beefburgers

Preparation time
5 minutes

Cooking time
10 minutes

Makes 4

Calories
334 per portion

You will need
350 g / 12 oz extra lean minced
    beef
1 slice wholemeal bread, crusts
    removed and crumbled
1 egg, beaten
1 onion, peeled and finely
    chopped
1 teaspoon tomato purée
1 tablespoon soy sauce
salt and pepper
4 wholemeal baps, split
lettuce leaves
2 tomatoes, sliced
onion rings
watercress sprigs to garnish

Mix together the beef, crumbled bread, egg, onion, tomato purèe, soy sauce and salt and pepper to taste. Shape into four flat patties and arrange on the grill rack. Cook under a preheated moderate grill for 5–7 minutes on each side or according to taste.

Serve each burger in a wholemeal bap with lettuce, tomato and onion rings, garnished with watercress.

Cook's Tip

You can mince your own beef in a food processor. For the best results use lean cuts of meat, such as sirloin or rump steak, and mince the cubed meat in short bursts of the machine.

55 | *Mini Pasties*

Preparation time
10 minutes

Cooking time
15 minutes

Oven temperature
230C, 450F, Gas 8

Makes 8

Calories
229 per portion

You will need
2 teaspoons oil
1 onion, peeled and finely
    chopped
1 garlic clove, peeled and crushed
175 g / 6 oz extra lean minced
    beef
1 potato, peeled and grated
1 tablespoon soy sauce
1½ teaspoons tomato purée
salt and pepper
pinch dried mixed herbs
212-g / 7½-oz packet wholemeal
    or plain shortcrust pastry,
    thawed if frozen
1 tablespoon plain flour
1 egg, beaten, to glaze

Heat the oil and fry the onion for 2 minutes, stirring. Add the garlic and beef and stir-fry for 2 minutes until the beef is evenly coloured. Stir in the remaining ingredients and cook, stirring, for another minute. Remove from the heat.

Roll out the pastry on a lightly floured surface and cut into 5 cm / 2 inch squares. Moisten the edges of each square with egg, place a heaped teaspoon of the filling in the centre, fold the pastry over into a triangle and press the edges to seal. Cut a small slit in the top of each and brush with beaten egg.

Bake on the top shelf of a preheated oven for 10–12 minutes.

Serve hot with salad nibbles. Alternatively, cool on a wire tray and serve as an after-school snack.

56 | *Grilled Greek Pitta Pockets*

Preparation time
20 minutes

Cooking time
5–6 minutes

Serves 4

Calories
328 per portion

You will need
4 pitta breads
75 g / 3 oz cheese, grated

For the salad
100 g / 4 oz cooked lamb, finely
    shredded
50 g / 2 oz mushrooms, wiped
    and thinly sliced
1 small bunch spring onions,
    chopped
2 lettuce leaves, shredded
2 tomatoes, skinned, seeded and
    chopped
4 black olives, stoned and sliced
2–3 tablespoons yogurt salad
    dressing
salt and pepper

Cut a slit across the top of each pitta bread but not through to the base. Gently open out the bread through the slit to form a pocket.

To make the salad, mix the lamb with the mushrooms, onions, lettuce, tomatoes, olives, dressing, and salt and pepper to taste. Blend well.

Stuff the pitta pockets equally with the Greek salad and place on a grill rack. Sprinkle the cheese on top.

Place under a preheated moderate grill and cook for 5–6 minutes until golden and bubbly. Serve at once whole or cut through into halves.

Cook's Tip

When rolling out the pastry, only lightly flour the work surface and rolling pin. If you use too much flour, the cooked pastry will be hard and dry.

Cook's Tip

Pitta breads are oval shaped, flat loaves popular in Greece and Middle Mediterranean countries. They are made from plain and wholemeal flours, and are widely available from supermarkets.

57 | Quick-Fried Pizza

Preparation time
15 minutes

Cooking time
15 minutes

Serves 6

Calories
469 per portion

You will need
225 g / 8 oz self-raising flour
salt and pepper to taste
½ teaspoon mixed dried herbs
4 tablespoons olive oil
4 tablespoons water
4 tablespoons tomato purée
225 g / 8 oz tomatoes, skinned
    and thickly sliced
2 teaspoons chopped fresh basil
    or parsley
225 g / 8 oz salami, rinded and
    thinly sliced
12 stuffed olives, sliced
100 g / 4 oz Gruyère cheese, thinly
    sliced

Sift the flour and salt and pepper together, then stir in the herbs. Stir in 2 tablespoons of the oil and the water and mix to form a soft dough. Knead on a lightly floured surface until smooth. Roll out the dough to form a 23 cm / 9 inch circle.

Heat one tablespoon of the remaining oil and cook the pizza base over moderate heat for 5 minutes. Remove the pizza from the pan, heat the remaining oil and return the pizza to cook the other side for 5 minutes.

Remove the pan from the heat. Spread the tomato purée over the top and cover it with sliced tomatoes. Sprinkle on the herbs. Arrange the salami in overlapping rings, with the olives between them. Arrange the cheese slices on top.

Cook the pizza under a preheated hot grill for 5 minutes, or until the cheese is browned. Serve hot.

Cook's Tip

For an Italian touch to this pizza, replace the Gruyère cheese with Mozzarella. This is a quick-melting cheese made from cow's milk. It is sold in small plastic bags with whey that has to be drained off before use.

58 | French Bread Pizza Toppers

Preparation time
15 minutes

Cooking time
12–14 minutes

Serves 4

Calories
282 per portion

You will need
1 large long French stick
3 tablespoons tomato purée
1 × 225-g / 8-oz can tomatoes,
    drained and chopped
1 teaspoon dried oregano or
    marjoram
salt and pepper
100 g / 4 oz Cheddar Cheese,
    grated
2 × 50-g / 2-oz cans anchovy
    fillets in oil, well drained
few black olives to garnish

Slice the French stick in half horizontally and lengthways. Place under a preheated hot grill and toast until golden.

Spread the bread with tomato purée. Top with the tomatoes, herbs, salt and pepper to taste and cheese. Arrange the anchovy fillets in a lattice over the cheese and garnish with the olives.

Place under a preheated moderate grill and cook for 10 minutes until golden and bubbly. Serve hot, cut into thick slices.

Cook's Tip

If the anchovy fillets are too salty, soak them in milk and cover for 10 minutes, then drain and arrange over the cheese. The milk removes some of the salt.

59 | Stuffed French Bread

Preparation time
25 minutes

Serves 3

Calories
631 per portion

You will need
1 large long crusty French stick
25 g / 1 oz butter, softened
2 lettuce leaves, shredded
3 slices Mortadella, rinded and rolled
25 g / 1 oz salami, rinded and rolled into cornets
50 g / 2 oz smoked cheese, rinded and sliced
50 g / 2 oz blue cheese, sliced
1 hard-boiled egg, shelled
1 large beefsteak tomato

For the coleslaw
100 g / 4 oz white cabbage, grated
25 g / 1 oz onion, grated
1 small carrot, grated
1 stick celery, chopped
1 tablespoon raisins
3 walnut halves, roughly chopped
3–4 tablespoons mayonnaise

To make the coleslaw, mix the cabbage with the onion, carrot, celery, raisins, walnuts and mayonnaise. Mix well.

Slice the loaf in half horizontally. Butter the inside of the loaf thinly. Spread the coleslaw along the length of the bottom half of the loaf and top with the lettuce, Mortadella, salami, smoked cheese, blue cheese, sliced egg and tomato, arranging attractively.

Press firmly together and cut vertically into 3 thick sections to serve.

Cook's Tip

Give this snack an Oriental flavour by substituting shredded Chinese leaves for the cabbage, bean-sprouts for the celery and water chestnuts for the onions. Water chestnuts are available canned in most supermarkets.

60 | Baked Continental Loaf

Preparation time
10 minutes

Cooking time
15–20 minutes

Oven temperature
190C, 375F, Gas 5

Serves 4

Calories
395 per portion

You will need
1 long crusty loaf of bread
50 g / 2 oz butter, softened
1 garlic clove, peeled and crushed
8 slices quick-melting cheese
8 slices cooked Continental-style ham
8 slices garlic sausage
2 tomatoes, thinly sliced

Make eight crosswise cuts equally along the length of the loaf almost to the base.

Cream the butter with the garlic and spread thinly between the slices of bread. Place a slice of cheese, ham, garlic sausage and tomato in each cut. Press gently together to re-form the loaf shape.

Cover the loaf loosely with foil. Place in a preheated oven and cook for 10–15 minutes.

Remove the top of the foil and cook for a further 5 minutes or until golden and bubbly. Pull apart or cut between the slices of bread to serve.

Cook's Tip

Using a wholemeal loaf of bread adds extra flavour as well as valuable dietary fibre.

61 | Fresh Herb Scones

Preparation time
15 minutes, plus resting

Cooking time
20 minutes

Oven temperature
220C, 425F, Gas 7

Makes 8

Calories
163 per portion

You will need
100 g / 4 oz wholemeal self-raising flour
100 g / 4 oz white self-raising flour
½ teaspoon salt
pepper
50 g / 2 oz hard vegetable margarine
2 tablespoons chopped fresh herbs such as parsley, sage, thyme, rosemary or 2 teaspoons mixed dried herbs
125 ml / 4 fl oz milk
1 tablespoon oil
milk for brushing
paprika to garnish

Mix together the flours, salt and pepper. Rub in the margarine until the mixture resembles fine breadcrumbs, then mix in the herbs. Make a well in the centre and slowly pour in the milk and oil, mixing to produce a soft dough.

Turn the dough onto a lightly floured surface and shape it into a ball, then flatten it gently to make a round about 15 cm / 6 inches across and 2½ cm / 1 inch thick.

Divide the round into 8 sections with a knife, cutting only halfway through the dough. Brush the top with milk and place on a floured baking sheet. Leave to rest for 15 minutes in a warm place.

Bake near the top of the oven for 20 minutes until well risen and golden brown. Remove from the oven and sprinkle with paprika. Cool on a wire tray. Serve cut into sections.

Cook's Tip

Using a combination of wholemeal and white flours makes the scones lighter than if they were made just with wholemeal flour. The hard vegetable margarine makes these savoury snacks suitable for serving to vegetarians.

62 | Scone and Bacon Roulade

Preparation time
15 minutes

Cooking time
30–35 minutes

Oven temperature
220C, 425F, Gas 7 then
190C, 375F, Gas 5

Serves 6

Calories
354 per portion

You will need
225 g / 8 oz self-raising flour
1 teaspoon baking powder
½ teaspoon salt
1–2 teaspoons mixed dried herbs
50 g / 20 oz butter, diced
1–2 tablespoons milk
2 tablespoons fruit chutney
100 g / 4 oz Cheddar cheese, grated
1 courgette, grated
1 stick celery, finely chopped
1 egg, beaten, to glaze
6 rashers back bacon, rinded

Sift the flour, baking powder and salt into a bowl, then stir in the herbs. Rub in the butter until the mixture resembles fine breadcrumbs. Mix in just enough milk to make a soft dough. Roll out on a lightly floured surface to a 20 × 30 cm / 8 × 12 inch rectangle.

Spread the chutney over the dough, leaving a border all round. Top with the cheese and vegetables. Moisten the edges with milk and roll up like a Swiss roll. Seal the edges and transfer to a baking sheet with the join underneath.

Brush with the egg, then make twelve slashes at regular intervals. Push a piece of bacon in each slash.

Bake in the centre of a preheated oven for 15–20 minutes until well risen, then cover with foil, lower the temperature and bake for a further 15 minutes, or until crusty and golden.

Serve hot or cold, cut into slices, on the day it is made.

Cook's Tip

If you have fresh herbs, substitute 1 tablespoon of a finely chopped selection for the dried. The easiest way to chop such a small amount is to hold the herbs over a bowl and snip them with a pair of scissors.

63 | Nut Savouries

Preparation time
8 minutes, plus chilling

Cooking time
12 minutes

Makes 12

Calories
117 per portion

You will need
2 onions, peeled and finely
   chopped
1 tablespoon tomato purée
1 garlic clove, peeled and crushed
2 slices wholemeal bread, crusts
   removed and made into crumbs
4 tomatoes, skinned and chopped
1 tablespoon chopped fresh
   parsley
salt and pepper
2 eggs, beaten
175 g / 6 oz almonds, hazelnuts or
   cashews, without skins and
   ground
wholemeal flour for coating
oil for frying
parsley sprigs to garnish

Mix together the onions, tomato purée and garlic, then add the breadcrumbs, tomatoes, parsley and salt and pepper to taste. Mix thoroughly, then stir in the eggs and nuts to make a sticky mixture. With lightly floured hands, shape into 12 hamburger shapes and coat with flour, shaking off excess. Chill for 30 minutes.

   Heat 2 tablespoons oil and lightly fry half the nut savouries for 3 minutes on each side. Keep warm while frying the remainder. Serve hot, garnished with parsley.

Cook's Tip

To remove the skins from almonds, put them in a heatproof bowl and cover with boiling water and leave for 2 minutes. Drain and plunge into cold water, then remove one by one and simply slide off the skins.

64 | Potato Pancakes with Green Sauce

Preparation time
15 minutes

Cooking time
10 minutes

Makes 8

Calories
317 per portion

You will need
6 potatoes, peeled and grated
2 eggs
1½ teaspoons salt
¼ teaspoon pepper
¼ teaspoon ground paprika
pinch ground mace
1 tablespoon plain flour
1 small onion, peeled and grated
oil for shallow frying
parsley sprigs to garnish

For the sauce
250 ml / 8 fl oz mayonnaise
1 teaspoon anchovy essence
3 spring onions, finely chopped
2 tablespoons chopped parsley
2 tablespoons chopped tarragon
1 tablespoon tarragon vinegar
150 ml / ¼ pint soured cream

Rinse the potatoes and pat dry with paper towels. Beat the eggs with the seasonings and flour, blending well. Stir in the grated onion and potato. Divide the mixture into 8 equal portions. Heat the oil and shallow fry the pancakes in two batches, flattening each slightly with a spatula, turning once. Cook for 5 minutes until crisp and golden. Drain well on paper towels and keep warm.

   Meanwhile, mix all the sauce ingredients, folding in the soured cream last. Chill until required. Serve the warm pancakes, garnished with parsley, with the chilled sauce on the side.

Cook's Tip

These crispy pancakes are ideal to serve as a starter for an informal dinner party with the sauce, or on their own as an accompaniment to roast chicken. The sauce can be made in advance and kept in the refrigerator.

Fish

Make the most of the wealth of fish and shellfish available today with these tempting and varied recipes. Included are dishes to serve as starters and main courses, as well as tasty salad ideas. Seafood has an important place in a healthy diet because most of it is usually high in protein and minerals and low in fat.

65 | Sole Normandie

Preparation time
10 minutes

Cooking time
15 minutes

Serves 4

Calories
503 per portion

You will need
4 sole fillets, skinned
150 ml / ¼ pint fish stock
75 g / 3 oz butter
100 g / 4 oz button mushrooms, wiped and sliced
40 g / 1½ oz plain flour
150 ml / ¼ pint milk
150 ml / ¼ pint double cream
600 ml / 1 pint cooked mussels, shelled
225 g / 8 oz cooked prawns, peeled
1 tablespoon chopped fresh parsley

Poach the fish in the stock for 8–10 minutes until cooked through and the flesh flakes when tested with the tip of a knife.

Meanwhile, melt half the butter and fry the mushrooms until tender and the excess liquid has evaporated.

Melt the remaining butter in another pan and stir in the flour. Cook for 3 minutes, then add the milk and cream. When the fish are poached, transfer to a warmed serving dish and keep warm. Add the poaching liquid to the sauce.

Cook the sauce until thickened, stirring. Stir in the mussels, prawns and mushrooms. Season to taste with salt and pepper.

Spoon the sauce over the fish and sprinkle with parsley.

Cook's Tip

If your fishmonger fillets the sole for you, be sure to ask for the skin and bones. These are excellent for making a delicately flavoured fish stock.

66 | Venetian Sole

Preparation time
20 minutes

Cooking time
15 minutes

Serves 4

Calories
689 per portion

You will need
4 Dover sole, about 350 g / 12 oz each, cleaned and skinned
100 g / 4 oz butter, softened
4 teaspoons chopped mint
4 teaspoons chopped parsley
2 garlic cloves, peeled and crushed
salt and pepper
parsley sprigs to garnish

For the sauce
50 g / 2 oz butter
2 shallots, peeled and finely chopped
225 ml / 8 fl oz dry white wine
125 ml / 4 fl oz double cream

Pat the sole dry. Make two or three diagonal slits in each side of the flesh. Blend the softened butter with the herbs, garlic and salt and pepper. Spread half the mixture equally over one side of each fish.

To make the sauce, melt the butter and fry the shallots for 5 minutes until softened. Stir in the wine, season to taste and cook for a further 2 minutes. Keep warm.

Place the fish, buttered side up, under a preheated moderate grill and cook for 3–4 minutes. Turn over, spread with remaining butter and cook for a further 3 minutes.

Stir the cream into the sauce and bring briefly to the boil. Place the fish on individual plates, spoon over a little sauce and garnish with parsley. Serve the remaining sauce separately.

Cook's Tip

Dover sole is considered the finest of the flat fish, highly prized for its flavour and delicate flesh. Consequently, it is very expensive. Lemon sole is an acceptable, less expensive alternative.

67 | Buttery Fried Plaice with Fried Parsley

Preparation time
10 minutes

Cooking time
20 minutes

Serves 6

Calories
532 per portion

You will need
plain flour for coating
salt and pepper
6 fillets of plaice, well trimmed
175 g / 6 oz butter
12 large parsley sprigs

Season the flour with the salt and pepper, then dip the fillets in it. Shake off any excess flour.

Melt half the butter and fry the fillets for 3 minutes on each side; if they are very large they may take a little longer. Add mcre of the butter if necessary, as flour-coated fish tends to soak up the fat. Remove from pan and keep warm on a serving platter. Fry in batches if necessary.

Add any remaining butter to the pan and raise the heat. Add the parsley and toss in the butter over a high heat, for 3–4 minutes until it becomes crispy.

Pour the parsley and juices over the fish and serve. Glazed carrots and baked potatoes are good accompanying vegetables.

Cook's Tip

This is a simple French way of pan-frying fish. The butter will become brown when frying the parsley but this adds an extra flavour. In France, it is called 'beurre noir', black butter.

68 | Plaice in Sweet and Sour Sauce

Preparation time
10 minutes

Cooking time
20 minutes

Serves 4

Calories
280 per portion

You will need
4 plaice fillets, about 175 g /6 oz each
100 g / 4 oz button mushrooms, wiped and sliced
1 red pepper, cored, seeded and very thinly sliced
2 tablespoons flaked almonds
1 tablespoon cornflour
4 tablespoons orange juice
grated rind of 1 orange
1 tablespoon light brown sugar
1 tablespoon clear honey
1 tablespoon cider vinegar
1 tablespoon tomato purée
1 tablespoon soy sauce
1 tablespoon sweet sherry
1 tablespoon oil
1 tablespoon Tabasco sauce

Cut four pieces of foil 20 × 30 cm / 8 × 12 inches and brush the centres with a little oil. Place each fillet on a piece of foil. Scatter the mushrooms, pepper and almonds over them. Bring up the sides of the foil and make a dish shape.

To make the sauce, put the cornflour into a bowl and gradually stir in the orange juice. Stir in the remaining ingredients with salt and pepper to taste.

Pour the sauce over the fish. Fold and seal the edges of the foil firmly to make watertight parcels. Place them in a steamer or colander over a pan of boiling water for 20 minutes, or until the fish flakes easily.

Cook's Tip

If you don't have a steamer or colander, the fish parcels can be cooked between two heatproof plates over a pan of boiling water. You will either have to cook the fish one at a time, or use four saucepans at once.

69 | *Plaice and Lime Pinwheels*

Preparation time
20 minutes

Cooking time
10–13 minutes

Makes 8

Calories
472 per portion

You will need
75 g / 3 oz butter, softened
2 tablespoons chopped fresh chives
40 g / 1½ oz fresh white breadcrumbs
grated rind of 1 lime
4 tablespoons lime juice
salt and pepper
8 plaice fillets, skinned

For the garnish
lime twists
fresh chives or dill

Beat the butter with the chives until soft and creamy. Add the breadcrumbs, lime rind and enough lime juice to make a stuffing with a good spreading consistency. Add salt and pepper to taste.

Divide the stuffing in four parts and spread the plaice fillets with the stuffing. Roll up from the wide end and secure each with a wooden cocktail stick.

Place in a greased flameproof dish and sprinkle with the remaining lime juice. Place under a preheated hot grill and cook for 5 minutes. Turn over and grill for a further 5–8 minutes. Serve at once garnished with lime twists and chives or dill.

70 | *Poached Trout*

Preparation time
5 minutes

Cooking time
10–12 minutes

Serves 4

Calories
312 per portion

You will need
4 rainbow trout, about 350 g / 12 oz each, cleaned
150 ml / ¼ pint dry cider
a few parsley stalks
1 onion, peeled and sliced
2 slices lemon
6 black peppercorns
150 ml / ¼ pint double cream
salt and pepper
parsley sprigs and lemon slices to garnish

Simmer the trout in the cider with the parsley stalks, onions, lemon and peppercorns, covered, for 10–12 minutes until the fish are just cooked and the flesh flakes easily. Transfer the fish to a serving plate and keep warm.

Strain the cooking liquid and bring it rapidly to the boil. Immediately lower the heat, stir in the cream and heat through. Remove from the heat and season with salt and pepper to taste.

Pour the sauce over the fish. Serve garnished with the parsley sprigs and lemon slices.

Cook's Tip

Use 1½ slices bread to make the breadcrumbs. Cut off the crusts and either process in a food processor or rub along a grater set in a bowl. You can also use wholemeal breadcrumbs.

Cook's Tip

If you decide to clean the fish yourself rather than having the fishmonger do it, wash out any blood along the back-bone. If not removed, the cooked fish can have a bitter taste.

71 | *Chilled Marinated Orange Trout*

Preparation time
15 minutes, plus
marinating

Cooking time
17–20 minutes

Serves 4

Calories
805 per portion

You will need
4 trout, about 350 g / 12 oz each,
   cleaned
seasoned plain flour
125 ml / 4 fl oz olive oil for frying
quartered orange slices to garnish

For the marinade
4 oranges
2 lemons
2 small onions, peeled and finely
   chopped
300 ml / ½ pint dry white wine
4 bay leaves
salt and pepper

Pat the trout dry with paper towels. Toss in seasoned flour, shaking off any excess. Heat all but 2 tablespoons oil and cook the trout for 12–15 minutes, turning once, until cooked through. Remove from the heat and drain on paper towels. When cold place on a serving dish.

Meanwhile, pare the rind from an orange and a lemon. Cut into thin matchstick strips. Place in a bowl, pour over boiling water and soak for 20 minutes. Squeeze the juice from the oranges and lemons and set aside.

Heat the remaining oil and fry the onions for 5 minutes until softened. Drain the orange and lemon strips, discard the liquid, and add strips to the pan with the orange and lemon juices, wine, bay leaves and salt and pepper to taste. Pour over the fish and leave to marinate for at least 6 hours. Serve garnished with orange slices.

Cook's Tip

While marinating the trout, make sure the dish is tightly covered with cling film or the fish may absorb other smells in the fridge and the delicate, citrus taste will be lost. Turn the trout over at least once while marinating.

72 | *Red Mullet with Tomato and Anchovy Sauce*

Preparation time
20 minutes

Cooking time
20 minutes

Serves 4

Calories
618 per portion

You will need
6 tablespoons olive oil
2 garlic cloves, peeled and
   crushed
2 × 225-g / 8-oz cans tomatoes
6 anchovy fillets, well drained and
   chopped
4 tablespoons chopped fresh
   parsley
pinch sugar
pepper
4 red mullet, about 450 g / 1 lb
   each, cleaned
salt
2 anchovy fillets, halved
   lengthways
parsley sprigs to garnish

Heat 4 tablespoons olive oil and fry the garlic until lightly coloured. Add the tomatoes, anchovies, parsley, sugar and pepper to taste. Bring to the boil, then simmer, uncovered, for 20 minutes until thickened.

Meanwhile, sprinkle the fish inside and out with salt and pepper. Brush the skin with the remaining olive oil. Make two diagonal slits in each side of the fish.
Place the fish under a preheated moderate grill for 7 minutes on each side.

Transfer the fish to individual plates and pour over some of the tomato mixture. Serve the remaining sauce separately. Garnish with anchovy strips and parsley.

Cook's Tip

Your fishmonger will scale the red mullet if you ask. To do it yourself, however, grip the fish by its tail. Using the back of a knife, scrape from the tail towards the head. Work over a sink because the scales fly everywhere.

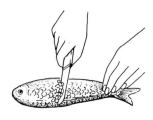

73 | Hake Paprika

Preparation time
15 minutes

Cooking time
30–35 minutes

Oven temperature
190C, 375F, Gas 5

Serves 4

Calories
286 per portion

You will need
75 g / 3 oz butter
2 large onions, peeled and sliced
3 canned pimientos, drained and
    chopped
4 hake portions, thawed if frozen
salt and pepper
300 ml / ½ pint plain yogurt
2 teaspoons paprika

For the garnish
croûtons
parsley sprigs

Melt 50 g / 2 oz of the butter and fry the onions for 5 minutes until softened. Add the pimientos and mix well.

Spoon half of the onion mixture into a greased ovenproof dish. Top with the fish and sprinkle with salt and pepper to taste. Dot with the remaining butter. Place in a preheated oven and cook, uncovered, for 15 minutes.

Top with the remaining onion mixture. Mix the yogurt with the paprika and pour over the fish. Bake for a further 10–15 minutes. Garnish with croûtons and parsley sprigs. Serve at once.

Cook's Tip

Substitute haddock or whiting portions for the hake. Using Greek yogurt will produce a richer sauce.

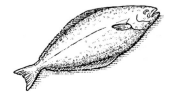

74 | Halibut with Raisins and Olives

Preparation time
10 minutes

Cooking time
20 minutes

Serves 4

Calories
428 per portion

You will need
4 small halibut steaks, or 2 large
    steaks, halved
seasoned plain flour
4 tablespoons olive oil for frying
2 garlic cloves, peeled and
    crushed
2 small onions, peeled and
    chopped
2 sticks celery, chopped
50 g / 2 oz seedless raisins
100 g / 4 oz stoned green olives
125 ml / 4 fl oz white wine
salt and pepper
celery leaves to garnish

Wash the halibut and pat dry with paper towels. Toss in seasoned flour, shaking off any excess.

Heat the oil and fry the fish for 10–12 minutes, turning once, until golden brown and cooked through. Transfer the fish to a serving plate and keep warm.

Add the garlic, onion and celery to the pan and fry for 5 minutes until softened. Add the raisins, olives, wine and salt and pepper to taste. Cook for a further 5 minutes.

Pour the sauce over the fish. Serve at once, garnished with celery leaves.

Cook's Tip

Halibut, a flat fish, has a firm but tender flesh. It can become dry, however, it is best to prepare this dish just before serving rather than trying to keep it warm for a long time.

75 | Salmon with Caper and Parsley Sauce

Preparation time
10 minutes

Cooking time
25 minutes

Serves 4

Calories
401 per portion

You will need
2 salmon steaks, 225 g / 8 oz each
salt and pepper
300 ml / ½ pint dry white wine
2 bay leaves
2 shallots, peeled and chopped
2 celery sticks, chopped
celery leaves to garnish

For the sauce
50 g / 2 oz butter
2 garlic cloves, peeled and
    crushed
2 tablespoons capers, drained and
    chopped
4 tablespoons chopped fresh
    parsley

Wipe the salmon steaks and sprinkle on both sides with salt and pepper. Place the wine, bay leaves, shallots and celery in a shallow pan and bring to a simmer. Add the salmon steaks, cover and poach for 12–15 minutes until the fish is cooked through.

Remove the salmon from the liquid, place on a warmed serving plate and keep warm. Strain the liquid and reserve.

To make the sauce, melt the butter and cook the garlic, capers and parsley for 1 minute. Add salt and pepper to taste and 125 ml / 4 fl oz of the poaching liquid. Bring to the boil. Pour over the salmon and serve at once, garnished with celery leaves.

Cook's Tip

The salmon steaks are cooked through when the flesh flakes easily if tested with the tip of a knife. Do not poach in boiling water or the cooked fish will be tough.

76 | Chilled Salmon Steaks

Preparation time
15 minutes

Cooking time
20 minutes

Oven temperature
180C, 350F, Gas 4

Serves 4

Calories
501 per portion

You will need
4 salmon steaks, 175 g / 6 oz each
salt and pepper
1 lemon
4 sprigs parsley or dill
4 tablespoons dry white wine
1 small cucumber, diced
about 150 ml / ¼ pint mayonnaise

For the garnish
lettuce
dill or parsley sprigs

Put the salmon steaks in a greased ovenproof dish and sprinkle with salt and pepper.

Grate the rind from the lemon and reserve for the sauce. Thinly slice the lemon and place one slice on top of each steak. Place a herb sprig on top of each salmon steak and pour the wine over. Cover the dish with foil and bake in a preheated oven for 20 minutes until the salmon is cooked but not dry. Leave to cool.

To make the sauce, place the cucumber in a bowl. Stir in the mayonnaise with any salmon cooking liquid, the reserved lemon rind and salt and pepper to taste. Add more mayonnaise if you want a larger quantity of sauce.

To serve, carefully remove the skin and the central bone from the salmon, keeping the steaks whole. Arrange the steaks on individual serving plates. Spoon cucumber sauce over each salmon steak where the bone has been removed. Garnish with lettuce and herbs.

Cook's Tip

This chilled fish dish is ideal for summer entertaining. The salmon steaks and poaching liquid can be kept separately, covered, in the refrigerator for a day. For variety, use halibut, cod or turbot instead of salmon.

77 | Marinated Mackerel

Preparation time
10 minutes, plus
cooling and marinating

Cooking time
30 minutes

Oven temperature
180C, 350F, Gas 4

Serves 4

Calories
283 per portion

You will need
4 medium mackerel, heads
    removed, gutted and cleaned
150 ml / ¼ pint dry cider
150 ml / ¼ pint water
1 slice lemon
large parsley sprig
large thyme sprig
1 bay leaf
salt and pepper

For the garnish
1 tablespoon chopped fresh
    parsley
1 tablespoon chopped fresh
    chives
sliced cucumber or shredded
    lettuce

Place the mackerel in an ovenproof dish or roasting tin. Pour over the cider and water and add the lemon, herbs, salt and pepper.

Cover and cook in a preheated oven for 20–30 minutes until tender and flesh flakes easily.

Remove the fish and set aside to cool. Remove the skin. Meanwhile, pour the cooking liquid into a saucepan and boil to reduce to about 150 ml / ¼ pint.

Place the mackerel in a shallow serving dish and pour over the reduced liquid. Cover and leave to marinate in a cool place for up to one day.

To serve, sprinkle with the chopped parsley and chives, and garnish with cucumber or lettuce.

Cook's Tip

Mackerel is an oily fish, and is ideal for marinating. Many supermarkets stock prepared fish, or your local fishmonger will remove the head and insides. It is very difficult to remove the skins before the fish are cool.

78 | Mackerel with Gooseberries

Preparation time
10 minutes

Cooking time
25 minutes

Oven temperature
180C, 350F, Gas 4

Serves 4

Calories
229 per portion

You will need
2 large mackerel, about 350 g /
    12 oz each, filleted
100 g / 4 oz gooseberries, topped
    and tailed
150 ml / ¼ pint dry cider
150 ml / ¼ pint milk
salt and pepper
1 tablespoon butter
1 tablespoon plain flour

Put the mackerel fillets into a shallow ovenproof dish with the gooseberries. Pour over the cider and milk and add salt and pepper to taste. Cover with foil and cook in a preheated oven for 20 minutes.

Carefully strain off the liquid, then keep the fish and gooseberries warm.

Melt the butter, stir in the flour and cook for 2–3 minutes. Pour in the cooking liquid and bring to the boil, stirring well, then cook for 2–3 minutes. Pour the sauce over the fish. Serve with new potatoes.

Cook's Tip

This recipe has a classic combination of flavours with the tartness of the gooseberries countering the richness of the mackerel. For extra flavour, add a pinch of ground ginger to the sauce.

79 | Mackerel with Cherries

Preparation time
5 minutes

Cooking time
10 minutes

Serves 4–6

Calories
284 per portion

You will need
100–175 g / 4–6 oz red cherries,
 stoned and chopped
4 tablespoons red wine
4 tablespoons water
1–2 teaspoons sugar
4–6 fresh mackerel fillets
pepper
lemon twists and parsley sprigs to
 garnish

Simmer the cherries in the wine and water for 10 minutes until soft. Add sugar to taste keeping the flavour tart. Cool for 1 minute, then purée in a liquidizer or food processor or mash with a fork. Return to the pan and keep warm while cooking the fish.

Meanwhile, season the mackerel with pepper to taste and cook under a preheated low grill for 5 minutes on each side until cooked through and the flesh flakes easily.

Transfer to warmed serving plates and serve at once with the hot cherry sauce, garnished with lemon and parsley.

Cook's Tip

When cherries aren't in season, use a 425-g / 15-oz can of red cherries, well drained. If they are too sweet, omit the sugar from the sauce and add 1–2 teaspoons lemon juice instead.

80 | Honey and Vegetable Mackerel

Preparation time
15 minutes

Cooking time
30 minutes

Oven temperature
190C, 375F, Gas 5

Serves 2

Calories
725 per portion

You will need
2 mackerel, about 450 g / 1 lb
 each, cleaned and heads
 removed
2 tablespoons clear honey
1 carrot, peeled and cut into
 matchstick strips
1 stick celery, cut into matchstick
 strips
1 × 5 cm / 2 inch slice fresh root
 ginger, peeled and cut into
 matchstick strips
salt and pepper
1 tablespoon wine vinegar
1 tablespoon soy sauce

Place the mackerel on a large piece of greased foil. Brush with the honey and sprinkle with the carrot, celery and ginger. Sprinkle with salt and pepper to taste, the wine vinegar and soy sauce.

Fold over the foil to enclose the fish completely, then place on a baking sheet. Place in a preheated oven and cook for 30 minutes or until tender. Remove from the foil to serve.

Cook's Tip

The fish packets can be prepared in advance and kept in the refrigerator until ready to cook. Crimp the edges of the foil tightly so none of the delicious juices ooze out.

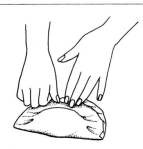

81 | *Smoked Mackerel and Orange Kebabs with Rice*

Preparation time
5 minutes

Cooking time
10 minutes

Serves 4

Calories
184 per portion

You will need
1 × 175-g / 6-oz packet par-cooked long-grain rice
salt
1 tablespoon butter
juice and grated rind of ½ orange
4 smoked mackerel fillets, about 175 g / 6 oz each, skinned
1 teaspoon lemon juice
pepper
3 large oranges, peeled and segmented
2 tablespoons blanched almonds, toasted
1 bunch watercress, trimmed to garnish

Cook the rice in boiling, salted water for 10 minutes, or until just tender. Drain and stir in the butter, orange juice and orange rind. Keep warm.

Meanwhile, cut the mackerel fillets crosswise into 2.5 cm / 1 inch strips and toss in the lemon juice. Sprinkle with pepper.

Thread the mackerel strips and orange segments alternately on to four skewers. Grill on a preheated hot grill for 5 minutes, turning the skewers once.

Just before serving, stir the toasted almonds into the rice. Serve the fish skewers on the rice, garnished with watercress sprigs.

Cook's Tip

To toast the almonds, place them in a single layer on a baking sheet under a hot grill for about 2 minutes, until golden. Use a long-handled wooden spoon to stir at least once.

82 | *Smoked Haddock Mousse*

Preparation time
20 minutes, plus chilling

Cooking time
12 minutes

Serves 4

Calories
275 per portion

You will need
450 g / l lb smoked haddock fillets, broken into pieces
300 ml / ½ pint milk
pepper
25 g / 1 oz butter
25 g / 1 oz plain flour
150 ml / ¼ pint double cream
2 tablespoons chopped fresh parsley
3 tablespoons dry white wine
15 g / ½ oz gelatine
1 tablespoon lemon juice
few drops anchovy essence
cucumber slices to garnish

Poach the haddock in the milk and pepper for 6–8 minutes until tender. Remove the haddock from the liquid and discard the skin and any bones. Reserve 150 ml / ¼ pint poaching liquid. Melt the butter, then stir in the flour and cook for 3 minutes, stirring. Add the reserved liquid and cream and continue cooking until the sauce boils and thickens. Add the parsley and haddock.

Meanwhile, place the wine in a small bowl and sprinkle the gelatine on top. Place in a pan of simmering water until the gelatine dissolves. Stir in the lemon juice, anchovy essence and pepper to taste, then fold into the fish mixture.

Spoon into a wetted 1.2 litre / 2 pint mould. Smooth the surface, then cover with cling film and chill until set.

To serve, unmould and garnish with cucumber slices.

Cook's Tip

To unmould, place a serving plate on top of the mould and turn over, giving a sharp shake halfway over. If not unmoulded, dip the mould in hot water. Do not leave for more than a few seconds or the design will disappear.

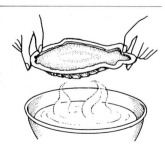

83 | *Parmesan Smokies*

Preparation time
10 minutes

Cooking time
20–25 minutes

Oven temperature
200C, 400F, Gas 6

Serves 4

Calories
479 per portion

You will need
450 g / 1 lb Arbroath Smokies,
   boned and skinned
300 ml / ½ pint water
1 fresh tarragon sprig
50 g / 2 oz butter
50 g / 2 oz plain flour
300 ml / ½ pint milk
150 ml / ¼ pint single cream
4 tablespoons dry white wine
50 g / 2 oz Cheddar cheese,
   grated
50 g / 2 oz Parmesan cheese,
   grated
salt and pepper
25 g / 1 oz fine fresh breadcrumbs

Poach the fish with the water and tarragon for 5 minutes until tender. Remove from the liquid and finely flake. Reserve 150 ml / ¼ pint poaching liquid.

Melt the butter and stir in the flour. Cook for 3 minutes, stirring, then stir in the milk, poaching liquid and cream and continue cooking, without boiling, until the sauce thickens.

Remove from the heat and stir in the fish, wine, Cheddar cheese and half the Parmesan cheese. Season to taste. Spoon into individual ovenproof dishes and top with the breadcrumbs and remaining cheese.

Cook for 10–15 minutes until golden and crisp. Serve at once.

84 | *Fried Whitebait*

Preparation time
10 minutes

Cooking time
12–15 minutes

Serves 4

Calories
715 per portion

You will need
500 g / 1 lb whitebait
100 g / 4 oz plain flour
salt and pepper
oil for deep frying

For the garnish
1 lemon, quartered
watercress sprigs

Sort through the whitebait, discarding any crushed or broken ones.

Season the flour with salt and pepper to taste and put in a shallow plate. Heat the oil to 180–190C / 350–375F or until a cube of bread browns in 30 seconds. Take a quarter of the fish and toss them in the flour, making sure they are well covered. Shake off any surplus flour and fry for 2 minutes. Drain the fish on paper towels and fry the remaining three batches.

When all the fish are cooked, check the oil temperature, re-heat and crisp all the whitebait for 2 minutes. Drain again, then pile them on to a serving dish and garnish with lemon and watercress. Serve as a starter with thin brown bread and butter if liked.

Cook's Tip

Arbroath Smokies are small, lightly smoked Scottish haddock, highly praised for their fine flavour and texture. If unavailable, smoked haddock is a good substitute.

Cook's Tip

Whitebait are miniature oily fish eaten whole, including the heads. To make a spicier dish, stir paprika or cayenne pepper to taste into the seasoned flour. If the fish need washing, use ice cold water and pat dry.

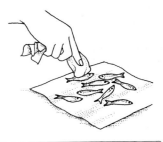

85 | Stuffed Sardines

Preparation time
10 minutes

Cooking time
6–8 minutes

Makes 6

Calories
236 per portion

You will need
350 g / 12 oz sardines, cleaned
salt and pepper
lemon wedges and parsley sprigs
  to garnish

For the stuffing
4 tablespoons chopped fresh
  parsley
50 g / 2 oz breadcrumbs
1 tablespoon lemon juice
1 tablespoon grated Parmesan
  cheese
25 g / 1 oz butter, melted
salt and pepper

Wash the sardines and pat dry. Sprinkle well with salt and pepper.

To make the stuffing, mix together the parsley, bread-crumbs, lemon juice, Parmesan cheese, butter and salt and pepper to taste.

Fill the cavity of each fish with a little stuffing.

Place the sardines under a preheated hot grill for 6–8 minutes, turning once, until cooked through and flesh flakes easily.

Cook's Tip

The stuffing can be made a day ahead but do not stuff the sardines until ready to grill. Leaving the fish overnight with the stuffing inside can be a health hazard, even if the fish are in the refrigerator.

86 | Seafood Casserole

Preparation time
10 minutes

Cooking time
20–25 minutes

Serves 4

Calories
191 per portion

You will need
4 tablespoons olive oil
2 garlic cloves, peeled and
  crushed
2 onions, peeled and chopped
2 small red peppers, cored,
  seeded and chopped
900 g / 2 lb mixed seafood, cut
  into pieces or steaks
4 tomatoes, skinned and sliced
300 ml ½ pint white wine
100 g / 4 oz whole button
  mushrooms, wiped
salt and pepper
toasted French bread to serve

Heat the oil and gently fry the garlic and onions for 5 minutes. Add the red peppers and cook for 2 minutes. Add the fish and stir to coat in oil.

Add the tomatoes, wine, mushrooms and salt and pepper to taste. Bring to the boil, then simmer, uncovered, for 15–20 minutes until the fish is tender.

Serve hot with toasted French bread and a salad.

Cook's Tip

The key to success with this Mediterranean-style recipe is to use a variety of seafood, including shellfish and firm white fish. Red mullet, scampi, cod, hake, sole and prawns are all ideal.

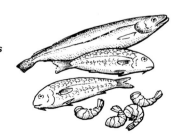

87 | Scallop Shells

Preparation time
10 minutes

Cooking time
15 minutes

Serves 4

Calories
274 per portion

You will need
2 tablespoons oil
1 small onion, peeled and finely
  chopped
1–2 garlic cloves, peeled and
  crushed
8–10 large scallops, removed from
  shells
1 tablespoon plain flour
salt and pepper
225 g / 8 oz button mushrooms,
  wiped and quartered
1 tablespoon lemon juice
4–5 tablespoons fine white
  breadcrumbs
3 tablespoons chopped fresh
  parsley

Heat the oil and fry the onion and garlic for 3 minutes until
softened.

Meanwhile, separate the orange roes from the scallops, then cut each scallop horizontally in half. Lightly
dust with the flour and season to taste with the salt and
pepper.

Add the scallops to the mushrooms and cook for 5–6
minutes until tender, then add the roes and lemon juice.
Cook for a further 3 minutes, stirring gently.

Heat the remaining oil, and fry the breadcrumbs for 3
minutes until crisp. Stir in the parsley.

To serve, spoon the scallop mixture into four heated
scallop shells and top with the crisp crumbs. Serve at
once.

88 | Moules à la Crème

Preparation time
15 minutes

Cooking time
20 minutes

Serves 4

Calories
353 per portion

You will need
2.25 litres / 4 pints fresh mussels,
  well scrubbed
300 ml / ½ pint water
2 tablespoons oil
25 g / 1 oz butter
2 onions, peeled and chopped
2 garlic cloves, peeled and
  crushed
150 ml / ¼ pint dry white wine
2 tablespoons chopped fresh
  parsley (optional)
150 ml / ¼ pint double cream
salt and pepper
parsley sprigs to garnish

Place the mussels and water in a large saucepan, cover
and cook over a high heat for 5–6 minutes until all the
shells open. Discard any that do not open.

Strain the mussels, reserving the cooking liquid. Remove and discard the mussels' top shells.

Heat the oil and butter and fry the onions and garlic for
5 minutes until soft. Add 150 ml / ¼ pint reserved liquid
and cook for a further 8 minutes.

Add the wine and parsley if liked. Bring almost to the
boil, then return the mussels and add the cream. Warm
through and season to taste with salt and pepper. Serve
in individual bowls, garnished with parsley sprigs.

Cook's Tip

*If your scallops aren't sold
with their shells, ask a
fishmonger if he has any
spare. Scrub them well before
using. You can also buy
scallop shells in cookware
shops. Alternatively, use
individual ramekins.*

Cook's Tip

*Place an empty bowl on the
table for everyone to put the
shells in as they eat the
mussels. The mussels can be
eaten with a fork or scooped
out of the half shells with
another shell, used as a
spoon. Give everyone a soup
spoon for eating the sauce at
the bottom of the bowl.
Finger bowls for cleaning your
hands are also useful.*

Poultry

Poultry has a well deserved reputation for versatility and it is becoming even more popular with cooks concerned about healthy eating. With the skin removed, chicken and other poultry is a low-fat source of protein. The following selection offers recipes for main courses and salads, suitable for both informal meals and for entertaining.

89 | Arctic Chicken with Prawns

Preparation time
5 minutes

Cooking time
25–30 minutes

Serves 6

Calories
296 per portion

You will need
25 g / 1 oz butter
3 tablespoons oil
6 part-boned chicken breasts, about 175 g / 6 oz each
225 g / 8 oz mushrooms, wiped
1 tablespoon lemon juice
150 ml / ¼ pint soured cream
225 ml / 8 fl oz dry white wine
225 g / 8 oz peeled cooked prawns
salt and pepper
parsley sprigs and chopped parsley to garnish

Heat the butter and oil and fry the chicken for 12–15 minutes until golden brown and tender. Transfer to a heated serving dish and keep warm.

Put the mushrooms and lemon juice in the pan and toss in the butter and oil mixture for 30 seconds, then stir in the soured cream and wine. Heat for 10 minutes, without boiling, stirring occasionally.

Add most of the prawns and salt and pepper to taste. Heat through, then spoon over the chicken.

Serve at once, garnished with the reserved prawns and parsley.

90 | Stuffed Chicken Breasts

Preparation time
15 minutes

Cooking time
35 minutes

Oven temperature
200C, 400F, Gas 6

Serves 4

Calories
437 per portion

You will need
4 chicken breasts, about 150 g / 5 oz each
75 g / 3 oz butter, softened
100 g / 4 oz cooked ham, finely chopped
2 garlic cloves, peeled and crushed
2 tablespoons grated Parmesan cheese
1 teaspoon fresh or dried rosemary, chopped
salt and pepper
6 tablespoons dry white wine

Wipe the chicken breasts with paper towels. Loosen the skin from the breast.

Beat 50 g / 2 oz of the butter with the ham, garlic, Parmesan cheese, rosemary and salt and pepper to taste. Spread the stuffing under the skin of each chicken breast and secure with wooden cocktail sticks.

Place the chicken in an ovenproof dish, dot with the remaining butter and sprinkle with salt and pepper. Cook in a preheated oven for 30 minutes until tender, golden brown and cooked through.

Place the chicken on individual plates. Pour the pan juices into a small saucepan, add the wine and bring to the boil, then simmer for 2 minutes. Add more salt and pepper if necessary. Pour the sauce over the chicken.

Cook's Tip

To lower the fat content of this dish, remove the skin from the chicken breast before cooking. Without the skin, chicken is low in fat and high in protein.

Cook's Tip

Use your fingers to gently ease the chicken skin away from the flesh to create a 'pocket' for the stuffing. Take care that your nails don't tear the skin.

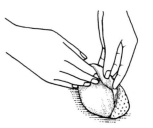

91 | *Chicken in Mushroom Sauce*

Preparation time
5 minutes

Cooking time
15 minutes

Serves 6

Calories
214 per portion

You will need
6 chicken breasts, about 100 g / 4 oz each, skinned
25 g / 1 oz cornflour, sifted
2 tablespoons oil
watercress sprigs to garnish

For the sauce
2 teaspoons butter, softened
1 shallot, finely chopped
175 g / 6 oz mushrooms, wiped and finely chopped
6 tablespoons single cream
75 ml / 3 fl oz cold water
¼ teaspoon French mustard
1 teaspoon soy sauce
1 teaspoon cornflour
salt and pepper

Dust the chicken with the cornflour until well coated. Shake off any excess.

Heat the oil and gently fry the chicken breasts for 5 minutes on each side, or until cooked through. Drain well on paper towels and keep warm.

To make the sauce, melt the butter and stir-fry the shallots and mushrooms for 1 minute. Put the cream, water, mustard, soy sauce and cornflour in a small bowl and mix until smooth, then add to the mushroom mixture and cook, stirring, until the mixture has thickened. Season with salt and pepper to taste.

Spoon the sauce over the chicken and serve, garnished with watercress.

Cook's Tip

Do not boil the sauce after the cream has been added or it may curdle. If you do not have a shallot, substitute 1 small onion.

92 | *Quick Coq au Vin*

Preparation time
7 minutes

Cooking time
7 minutes

Serves 4

Calories
223 per portion

You will need
1 tablespoon oil
1 onion, peeled and finely chopped
2 garlic cloves, peeled and crushed
2–3 chicken breasts, about 100 g / 4 oz each, skinned and cut into matchstick strips
2 slices lean cooked ham, cut into matchstick strips
6 tablespoons dry red wine
1 tablespoon soy sauce
salt and pepper
French bread slices to serve

Heat the oil and fry the onion for 3 minutes. Stir in the garlic, then push the mixture to one side of the pan. Tilt the pan to let the juices run out of the onions and over the base.

Add the chicken pieces and stir-fry over a high heat for 2 minutes until lightly coloured. Stir into the onions, then add the ham, wine, soy sauce and salt and pepper to taste and heat through gently.

Serve hot with thick slices of French bread, fried in oil on one side only, until crisp and golden.

Cook's Tip

Serve this flavourful stir-fried dish with a robust bottle of red wine, such as a Burgundy. Burgundy is a region in France where the original version of this dish was made famous.

93 | Grilled Chicken with Cheese

Preparation time
5 minutes

Cooking time
35 minutes

Serves 4

Calories
361 per portion

You will need
4 boneless chicken breasts, skinned
4 tablespoons vegetable oil
1 tablespoon lemon juice
1 teaspoon dried thyme
salt and pepper
100 g / 4 oz cooked ham, thinly sliced
50 g / 2 oz Gruyère cheese, thinly sliced
2 large tomatoes

Cut four pieces of foil about 30 cm / 12 inches square. Cut three slits in each chicken breast and lay on the foil.

Mix together the oil, lemon juice, thyme and salt and pepper to taste. Draw the foil around the chicken, pour on the sauce and seal the parcels.

Cook the chicken parcels under a preheated moderate grill, turning them once, for 30 minutes until the juices run clear when the chicken pieces are pierced with a skewer. Increase the heat to high.

Open the parcels, arrange the sliced ham, then cheese, then tomatoes on the chicken breasts and spoon a little sauce on to the tomatoes. Grill the topping under high heat for 3–4 minutes until the cheese is bubbling. Serve at once.

Cook's Tip

If you have an electric grill take extra care that the foil does not touch the heating element or sparks will fly.

94 | Chicken and Rice

Preparation time
6 minutes

Cooking time
8 minutes

Serves 4–6

Calories
122 per portion

You will need
1 tablespoon oil
1 onion, peeled and finely chopped
1 garlic clove, peeled and crushed
50 g / 2 oz mushrooms, wiped and chopped
150–175 g / 5–6 oz cooked boneless chicken, skinned and chopped
1 tablespoon soy sauce
salt and pepper
150–200 g / 5–7 oz rice, cooked
2 tomatoes, skinned and chopped
1 tablespoon chopped fresh parsley
juice of ½ lemon
parsley sprigs and lemon twists to garnish

Heat the oil and fry the onion, stirring occasionally, for 3 minutes until softened. Add the garlic, mushrooms, chicken, soy sauce and salt and pepper to taste and stir-fry for 3 minutes.

Add the rice, tomatoes, parsley and lemon juice and heat gently, turning the mixture over with two large wooden spoons. When the rice is heated through, transfer the mixture to warmed serving plates. Serve hot, garnished with parsley and lemon.

Cook's Tip

Any type of rice is suitable for this dish, except the short-grained pudding rice. For an Italian touch, use arborio rice, the rice used in risottos. It has the advantage of not breaking up when stirred.

95 | *Chicken Satay*

Preparation time
10 minutes

Cooking time
15–20 minutes

Serves 4–6

Calories
238 per portion

You will need
750 g / 1½ lb boneless chicken, skinned and cubed
2 garlic cloves, peeled and crushed
1 tablespoon oil
½ tablespoon vinegar
4 tablespoons water

For the sauce
1 garlic clove, peeled and crushed
4 tablespoons peanut butter
75 ml / 3 fl oz coconut milk
¼–½ teaspoon chilli powder
1–2 teaspoons soy sauce
1 bay leaf
1 teaspoon brown sugar
salt and pepper

Place the chicken on kebab skewers. Place in a glass bowl that will hold the skewers in a single layer.

Mix together the garlic, oil, vinegar and water, then pour over the chicken. Cover and marinate while preparing the sauce.

To make the sauce, mix all the ingredients together and simmer for 10 minutes, stirring occasionally, until well blended. Remove the bay leaf.

Cook the chicken under a preheated hot grill, turning and basting with any remaining marinade, until cooked through. Place on a warmed serving dish with the sauce served separately.

96 | *Parmesan Chicken Drumsticks*

Preparation time
15 minutes, plus chilling

Cooking time
15–20 minutes

Serves 4

Calories
298 per portion

You will need
50 g / 2 oz fresh white breadcrumbs
50 g / 2 oz Parmesan cheese, finely grated
2 tablespoons plain flour
salt and pepper
2 eggs, beaten
8 large chicken drumsticks, skinned

Mix the breadcrumbs and Parmesan cheese together in a bowl. Season the flour with salt and pepper to taste and put on a plate. Put the eggs in another bowl.

Coat the drumsticks with the seasoned flour, shaking off any excess, then dip in the egg and roll in the breadcrumbs. Chill for 30 minutes.

Cook under a preheated grill for 15–20 minutes, or until the drumsticks are cooked through and the juices run clear when pierced with the tip of a knife. Serve either hot or cold.

Cook's Tip

This Indonesian-style dish includes soy sauce, a popular ingredient in Asian cooking. It is made from soya beans and has a sharp, salty taste.

Cook's Tip

For a crunchy coating, replace the cheese with 50 g / 2 oz finely chopped peanuts. Served cold, either version is ideal for picnics or casual summer meals.

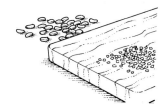

97 | Chicken Livers with Sage and Wine

Preparation time
10 minutes

Cooking time
15–18 minutes

Serves 4

Calories
196 per portion

You will need
750 g / 24 oz chicken livers, thawed if frozen, and trimmed
50 g / 2 oz butter
2 small onions, peeled and finely chopped
12 whole sage leaves, or 2 teaspoons dried
salt and pepper
300 ml / ½ pint dry white wine
sage leaves and orange slices to garnish

Pat the chicken livers dry with paper towels.

Melt the butter and fry the onion for 5–6 minutes until softened. Add the chicken livers and sage and fry for 3–4 minutes, stirring until the chicken livers have changed colour.

Sprinkle with salt and pepper to taste and pour in the wine. Bring to the boil, then simmer for 6–8 minutes until the chicken livers are tender.

Serve at once, garnished with sage and orange slices.

98 | Chicken Liver Ring

Preparation time
15 minutes, plus chilling and setting

Serves 4

Calories
161 per portion

You will need
1 × 25-g / 1-oz packet aspic jelly powder
600 ml / 1 pint water
2 tablespoons dry or medium sherry
25 g / 1 oz butter
225 g / 8 oz chicken livers, trimmed and roughly chopped
2 spring onions, thinly sliced
1 carton mustard and cress to garnish

Make up the aspic jelly with the water according to the packet instructions. Leave to cool until beginning to thicken but not set. Stir in the sherry.

Melt the butter and fry the chicken livers for 3 minutes, turning frequently, until cooked through. Drain on paper towels and allow to cool.

Pour 150 ml / ¼ pint of the aspic jelly into the base of a 900 ml / 1½ pint ring mould. Place in the refrigerator or freezer to set.

Sprinkle the spring onions on top of the set aspic jelly. Distribute the chicken livers in the ring mould, then pour in the remaining aspic jelly to fill up the mould. Place in the refigerator until set.

To serve, turn out and surround with a garnish of mustard and cress.

Cook's Tip

Thaw tubs of frozen chicken livers in the microwave oven without removing from the tub. Alternatively, place the frozen tub in a bowl of water at room temperature. Do not place in hot water; this would encourage bacterial growth.

Cook's Tip

When trimming the chicken livers, carefully remove any sections with a slight green tinge. If left on, the livers will taste very bitter.

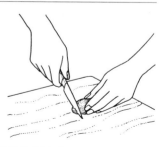

99 | Chicken with Piquant Green Sauce

Preparation time
10 minutes

Serves 4

Calories
261 per portion

You will need
4 cooked chicken breasts, about
   150 g / 5 oz each, skinned
lemon wedges to garnish

For the sauce
2 garlic cloves, peeled and
   crushed
2 tablespoons capers, drained and
   finely chopped
50 g / 2 oz fresh parsley, finely
   chopped
2 tablespoons wine vinegar
1 teaspoon Dijon mustard
75 ml / 3 fl oz olive oil
salt and pepper

To make the sauce, mix together the garlic, capers, parsley, vinegar and mustard. Gradually stir in the oil, then add salt and pepper to taste. Cover and chill until ready to serve.

   Slice the chicken breasts thinly and arrange on a serving dish. Pour a little sauce over each slice and serve any remaining separately. Garnish with lemon wedges.

100 | Chicken Salad Véronique

Preparation time
20 minutes

Cooking time
10 minutes

Serves 4

Calories
357 per portion

You will need
4 tablespoons cooking oil
1 garlic clove, peeled
4 boned chicken breasts
50 g / 2 oz split or flaked almonds
1 head endive to serve
225 g / 8 oz green grapes, halved,
   pips removed, or whole
   seedless grapes to garnish

For the dressing
150 ml / 5 fl oz soured cream
1 tablespoon white vermouth or
   dry white wine
salt and pepper

Heat the oil in a frying pan with the garlic. Fry the chicken on both sides for 5–10 minutes until golden brown and cooked through.

   Remove the chicken and drain on paper towels. Add the almonds to the pan and fry gently, stirring constantly, until lightly browned. Remove from the pan and drain. Cool the chicken and almonds. Reserve the cooking oil and cool, discarding the garlic.

   Spoon the soured cream into a bowl and beat in the cold cooking oil, vermouth or white wine, and salt and pepper to taste. Add a little more vermouth or white wine if a sharper dressing is preferred.

   Arrange a bed of endive on a serving dish and place the cold chicken breasts on top. Spoon the dressing over the chicken and scatter with almonds and grapes.

Cook's Tip

Serve this chilled chicken dish as part of a summer buffet. It goes well with a selection of lettuce salads and slices of wholemeal bread with unsalted butter.

Cook's Tip

When recipe titles include the word 'Véronique' it means they are garnished with green grapes. The best-known example is Sole Véronique, a French dish of sole fillets in a creamy white wine sauce with green grapes that is served hot. This cold dish is an excellent choice for a light lunch main course or as part of a buffet. The chicken and dressing can each be prepared in advance but the salad should be assembled just before serving.

101 | Summer Chicken

Preparation time
30 minutes, plus
marinating

Serves 4

Calories
438 per portion

You will need
450 g / 1 lb boneless cooked
  chicken
100 ml / 3½ fl oz dry white wine
1 teaspoon lemon juice
2 teaspoons grated onion
1 teaspoon chopped fresh
  tarragon
pinch onion salt
4 oranges, peeled and segmented
100 g / 4 oz small lettuce leaves or
  endive, rinsed
1 bunch watercress
50 g / 2 oz walnuts, toasted
thin strips orange rind to garnish

For the dressing
75 g / 3 oz full fat soft cheese
150 ml / ¼ pint soured cream
3 drops Tabasco sauce
salt and pepper

Thinly slice the chicken. Combine with the wine, lemon juice, onion, tarragon, onion salt and orange segments, blending well. Cover and marinate for 20 minutes.

Meanwhile, toss the lettuce or endive with the watercress and use to line a serving plate.

Remove the chicken and orange segments from the marinade and mix with the pine nuts, reserving the marinade. Spoon the chicken mixture on to the serving plate.

Mix the dressing ingredients, adding 1–2 tablespoons marinade to make a thick pouring consistency. Pour over the chicken mixture. Serve garnished with orange rind.

Cook's Tip

The orange segments can be replaced with pink grapefruit segments or sliced kiwi fruit if liked.

102 | Tropical Curried Chicken Salad

Preparation time
20 minutes

Serves 4

Calories
369 per portion

You will need
350 g / 12 oz cooked chicken,
  skinned and boned
2 bananas, sliced
1 tablespoon lemon juice
50 g / 2 oz cashew nuts
25 g / 1 oz raisins
50 g / 2 oz ready-to-eat dried
  apricots, roughly chopped
1 tablespoon long-thread coconut,
  toasted, to garnish

For the dressing
3 tablespoons mayonnaise
1 tablespoon finely chopped onion
½ teaspoon hot Madras curry
  powder
½ teaspoon lemon juice
2 tablespoons grated sweet apple
1 teaspoon mango chutney
pinch salt

To make the dressing, mix the mayonnaise with the onion, curry powder, lemon juice, apple, chutney and salt, blending well.

Cut the chicken into bite-sized pieces. Place in a serving bowl with the bananas and lemon juice, tossing gently to mix. Add the cashew nuts, raisins and dried apricots, blending well. Chill until ready to serve.

Just before serving, spoon the dressing over the salad ingredients and toss well to mix. Sprinkle with the toasted coconut.

Cook's Tip

Serve this salad with Poppadums, crisp, thin Indian wafers. They are available plain or spiced from supermarkets and Indian shops. The packet will give instructions for frying or grilling.

103 | Chicken, Tarragon and Orange Salad

Preparation time
15 minutes, plus chilling

Cooking time
15 minutes

Serves 4

Calories
461 per portion

You will need
600 ml / 1 pint chicken stock
grated rind and juice of 1 orange
1 tablespoon chopped fresh
   tarragon, or ½ tablespoon dried
1 bay leaf
salt and pepper
½–1 tablespoon wine vinegar
4 cooked boneless chicken
   breasts, skinned
lettuce leaves to serve

For the garnish
1 orange, peeled and sliced
1 carton mustard and cress
fresh tarragon sprigs (optional)

Boil the chicken stock, orange rind and juice, tarragon, bay leaf and a little salt and pepper together until reduced to 300 ml / ½ pint. Cool to room temperature, then refrigerate until any fat is set in a solid layer on top.

Meanwhile, cut the chicken into bite-sized pieces and place in a large bowl. Cover and refrigerate.

Remove the fat from the stock, then reheat the stock. Stir in the oil, vinegar and salt and pepper to taste. Pour this dressing over the chicken and mix well. Serve at once or cover and chill.

Serve the salad on a plate lined with lettuce leaves. Garnish with orange slices, cress and tarragon sprigs.

Cook's Tip

It is more economical to buy a whole chicken rather than pieces. If you want to use a whole bird, poach it in water to cover with the orange rind and juice, tarragon, bay leaf and 1 sliced onion. Use the cooking liquid for the stock.

104 | Duck, Red Cabbage and Roquefort Salad

Preparation time
10 minutes

Cooking time
15–20 minutes

Serves 4

Calories
554 per portion

You will need
2 large portions duck breast,
   about 450 g / 1 lb each
2 tablespoons clear honey
225 g / 8 oz red cabbage, thinly
   sliced
½ lettuce or endive, thinly sliced
225 g / 8 oz Roquefort cheese
4 tablespoons French dressing

Place the duck portions on a baking sheet and brush with the honey. Cook under a preheated moderate grill for 15 minutes, basting and turning, until they are cooked through and the skins are crispy and well browned. Leave to cool.

Divide the red cabbage and lettuce between four serving plates.

Thinly slice the duck breast and arrange on top of the cabbage and lettuce.

Cut the Roquefort cheese into small cubes and sprinkle over the top of the salad. Pour 1 tablespoon of French dressing over each salad plate before serving.

Cook's Tip

For a dinner party, the above recipe is sufficient for six people as a starter. It is also possible to substitute four small or two large chicken breasts for the duck, and Stilton cheese to replace the Roquefort cheese.

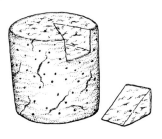

105 | Duck with Passion Fruit

Preparation time
7 minutes

Cooking time
7 minutes

Serves 4

Calories
109 per portion

You will need
1 tablespoon oil
1 onion, peeled and thinly sliced
1 garlic clove, peeled and crushed
2 duck breasts, about 450 g / 1 lb
   each, skinned and cut into thin
   slivers
1 passion fruit, halved and sieved
juice of 1 orange
2 teaspoons sugar
1 tablespoon soy sauce
2 teaspoons cornflour blended
   with 5 tablespoons water
salt and pepper
nasturtium flowers to garnish
   (optional)

Heat the oil and fry the onion for 2 minutes, stirring. Stir in the garlic, then push to one side of the pan. Tilt the pan to let the juices run out and over the base.

Increase the heat, add the duck and stir-fry for 3 minutes until no longer pink. Lower the heat and add the passion fruit, orange juice, sugar, soy sauce, blended cornflour and salt and pepper to taste, stirring until thickened.

Serve hot, garnished with nasturtium flowers.

Cook's Tip

Passion fruit is a tropical fruit now widely available. It is ready to use when the skin is hard, wrinkled and purple-brown. Cut in half and scoop out the seeds and pulp. For this recipe, sieve fruit through a fine nylon sieve.

106 | Braised Turkey Breast with Chestnuts

Preparation time
20 minutes

Cooking time
30 minutes

Serves 6

Calories
451 per portion

You will need
50 g / 2 oz butter
2 tablespoons oil
500 g / 1¼ lb turkey breast slices
2 onions, peeled and chopped
100 g / 4 oz streaky bacon, rinded
   and diced
1 tablespoon plain flour
300 ml / ½ pint chicken stock
150 ml / ¼ pint dry white wine
1 teaspoon dried tarragon
1 × 450-g / 1-lb can whole
   chestnuts, drained
3 tablespoons double cream
salt and pepper

Melt the butter and oil and fry the turkey breast slices for 2 minutes on either side until lightly browned. Remove them from the pan. Add the onions and bacon to the pan juices and fry gently, stirring, for 5 minutes.

Sprinkle in the flour and cook, stirring for 1 minute. Gradually stir in the stock and wine. Add the tarragon and chestnuts.

Return the turkey to the pan, making sure that the slices are well covered with sauce. Cook gently for 20 minutes, stirring occasionally.

Remove the turkey to a serving dish and keep warm.

Add the cream to the sauce with salt and pepper. Pour the sauce over the turkey slices and serve immediately.

Cook's Tip

Be careful when seasoning not to add too much salt. The bacon will add a salty taste and the cooked dish may not need any more salt.

107 | Turkey Escalopes with Anchovies

Preparation time
15 minutes, plus marinating

Cooking time
10 minutes

Serves 4

Calories
304 per portion

You will need
juice and grated rind of 1 lemon
2 tablespoons olive oil
1 teaspoon dried oregano
salt and pepper
450 g / 1 lb turkey breast slices
2 tablespoons plain flour
75 g / 3 oz fresh breadcrumbs
2 tablespoons chopped fresh mint
1 egg
1 tablespoon milk
1 tablespoon oil for frying

For the garnish
1 × 50-g / 2-oz can anchovy fillets, drained
8 stuffed olives
2 hard-boiled eggs, sliced

To make the marinade, mix together the lemon juice, olive oil, oregano and salt and pepper. Pour into a shallow dish and add the turkey breast slices. Cover and marinate for 1 hour, or overnight in the refrigerator, turning once.

Drain the meat and pat it dry. Season the flour with salt and pepper and put on a plate. Mix the breadcrumbs, lemon rind and mint together in a bowl. Beat the egg and milk together. Coat the turkey with the seasoned flour, then dip in the egg and roll in the breadcrumb mixture.

Heat the oil and fry the turkey slices for 3–4 minutes on each side until evenly browned. Arrange on a heated serving dish. Garnish with the anchovy fillets, each one rolled around an olive, and with egg slices.

Cook's Tip

If you have time, chill the coated turkey pieces for 30 minutes before frying. This helps to set the coating, so it is less likely to fall off during cooking.

108 | Turkey with Walnuts

Preparation time
10 minutes

Cooking time
6 minutes

Serves 4

Calories
115 per portion

You will need
1 tablespoon oil
1 onion, peeled and finely chopped
1 garlic clove, peeled and crushed
1 turkey breast, skinned, sliced and cut into small slivers
grated rind and juice of 1 orange
25 g / 1 oz walnut halves, chopped
1 tablespoon soy sauce
2 teaspoons cornflour, blended with 4 tablespoons water
1 teaspoon soft brown sugar
1 tablespoon finely chopped fresh parsley
salt and pepper
shredded orange rind to garnish

Heat the oil and fry the onion, stirring, for 2 minutes. Stir in the garlic and push the mixture to one side of the pan. Tilt the pan to let the juices run out over the base.

Add the turkey and stir-fry for 2 minutes. Remove with a slotted spoon, transfer to a serving dish and keep warm.

Add the orange rind and juice, walnuts, soy sauce, blended cornflour, sugar and parsley to the pan. Bring to the boil, stirring, then simmer until thickened. Stir in salt and pepper to taste and pour over the turkey. Serve hot, garnished with shredded orange rind.

Cook's Tip

This is a good dish to use up leftover turkey meat. If you do use cooked meat, make sure the skin and any small bones are removed. Stir-fry the onion and garlic for 3 minutes before adding the meat.

Meat and Offal

Beef, lamb, pork and offal each lend themselves to a variety of cooking techniques, so they can easily fit into a busy cook's schedule. Although meat is often an expensive ingredient, some of the lean, boneless cuts are quick to prepare and have little or no waste, so they may offer good value. These recipes include different cuts for every budget and taste.

109 | Steaks with Peppercorn Sauce

Preparation time
5 minutes

Cooking time
10–15 minutes

Serves 4

Calories
530 per portion

You will need
salt and pepper
4 rump or fillet steaks, about
    150 g / 5 oz each
50 g / 2 oz butter
2 tablespoons brandy
150 ml / ¼ pint double cream
2 tablespoons canned or bottled
    green or pink peppercorns
watercress sprigs to garnish

Sprinkle salt and pepper to taste on both sides of the steaks. Melt the butter, add the steaks and fry quickly on both sides until browned, 3–5 minutes each side according to taste.

Pour over the brandy, ignite and allow the flames to die down. Remove the steaks from the pan with a slotted spoon and place on a warmed serving dish.

Add the cream and peppercorns to the pan and cook for 1 minute or until lightly thickened. Spoon sauce over the steaks. Garnish with the watercress sprigs.

110 | Steak with Anchovies

Preparation time
5 minutes

Cooking time
8 minutes

Serves 4

Calories
456 per portion

You will need
750 g / 1½ lb rump steak, cut into
    4 pieces
pepper
40 g / 1½ oz butter, softened
1 tablespoon oil
1 tablespoon chopped fresh
    parsley
2 drops lemon juice
1 × 50-g / 2-oz can anchovy fillets,
    well drained

Snip the fat on the steak and grind pepper on to both sides. Melt 15 g / ½ oz of the butter with the oil and, when it is very hot, add the steak. Seal the steak on one side for 2 minutes, turn and seal on the other side for 2 minutes.

Reduce the heat to moderately hot and continue cooking for a further 1–3 minutes on each side, or until the steak is cooked as you like it.

Meanwhile, beat the remaining butter with the parsley, lemon juice and pepper to taste. Shape it into a roll and chill it in the freezing compartment of the refrigerator for a few minutes.

To serve, arrange the anchovy fillets on the steaks and, at the last moment, place pats of parsley butter on top.

Cook's Tip

A safe way to ignite the brandy is to put it in a ladle with a long handle. Hold the ladle over a gas flame and the brandy will burst into flames. Then pour it over the steaks. Protect your hand with an oven glove or pot-holder.

Cook's Tip

Cooking the steak on both sides in very hot fat seals the surfaces so none of the juices run out during the remaining cooking time. This keeps the steaks tender and adds extra flavour.

111 | *Marsala Steaks*

Preparation time
10 minutes

Cooking time
10–15 minutes

Serves 4

Calories
784 per portion

You will need
2 rump steaks, about 225 g / 8 oz
    each
salt and pepper
50 g / 2 oz butter
4 teaspoons olive oil
100 g / 4 oz mushrooms, wiped
    and finely chopped
50 g / 2 oz smooth pâté
4 tablespoons Marsala
6 tablespoons brandy
thyme sprigs to garnish

Sprinkle the steaks on both sides with salt and pepper to taste.

Heat the butter and oil and fry the steaks for 2–4 minutes on each side until browned and cooked to your liking. Keep warm.

Add the mushrooms to the pan and cook on a high heat for 1 minute, stirring constantly. Add the pâté and Marsala and stir until well mixed and hot. Add salt and pepper to taste and spread the mixture over the steaks. Return them to the frying pan.

Warm the brandy and pour over the steaks at the table. Carefully ignite the brandy and serve when the flames have extinguished. Garnish with sprigs of thyme.

112 | *Beef in Cream Sauce*

Preparation time
5 minutes

Cooking time
8 minutes

Serves 4

Calories
175 per portion

You will need
1 tablespoon oil
2 onions, peeled and thinly sliced
3–4 slices beef for beef olives, cut
    into matchstick strips
1 tablespoon soy sauce
2 tablespoons single cream
salt and pepper
parsley sprigs and tomato slices
    to garnish

Heat the oil and fry the onions for 4 minutes, stirring, until lightly browned. Push to one side of the pan. Tilt the pan to let the juices run out of the onions and over the base.

Add the meat strips and stir-fry for 2–3 minutes until evenly browned. Mix with the onions, then add the soy sauce and stir in the cream and salt and pepper to taste. Heat through gently, without boiling. Serve at once, garnished with parsley.

Cook's Tip

For variety, use sirloin steak instead of rump steak. Both cuts are tender and suitable for quick pan-frying.

Cook's Tip

Beef for beef olives are thin slices of lean beef available from supermarkets. These slices are usually rolled around a stuffing and braised. Otherwise, ask your butcher for beef suitable for quick cooking, such as topside.

113 | *Stir-fried Beef*

Preparation time
10 minutes, plus
marinating

Cooking time
20 minutes

Serves 4

Calories
419 per portion

You will need
450 g / 1 lb fillet of beef, thinly
   sliced
2 tablespoons soy sauce
4 teaspoons cornflour
salt
1 garlic clove, peeled and finely
   chopped
1 cm / ½ inch piece fresh root
   ginger, peeled and finely
   chopped
2 tablespoons oil
300 ml / ½ pint chicken stock
2 tablespoons dry sherry
6 tablespoons milk
8 spring onions, thinly sliced
spring onion tassels to garnish

Cut the beef into 1 cm / ½ inch wide strips. Mix together 1 tablespoon soy sauce, 1 teaspoon of the cornflour and a pinch of salt. Toss the beef in this marinade, cover and leave at room temperature for about 2 hours.

Heat the oil in a wok or large frying pan and fry the garlic and ginger over moderately high heat, stirring, for 1 minute. Add the stock, sherry and remaining soy sauce. Stir and bring to the boil, then lower the heat and simmer the sauce for 10 minutes.

Increase the heat again, add the beef, any marinade and the spring onions to the sauce. Stir-fry for 3 minutes. Pour the milk on to the remaining cornflour and stir to make a smooth paste. Add to the sauce, bring to the boil and stir-fry for 1–2 minutes until it thickens. Serve hot garnished with spring onion tassels.

Cook's Tip

Serve with tumeric-flavoured rice. Cook 175–225 g / 6–8 oz long-grain rice in boiling salted water with 1 teaspoon tumeric. Drain and keep hot until ready to serve. To make spring onion tassels curl decoratively, place in ice water for 5-10 minutes after slicing both ends.

114 | *Beef, Apricot and Apple Kebabs*

Preparation time
25 minutes

Cooking time
25–30 minutes

Makes 4

Calories
209 per portion

You will need
450 g / 1 lb thin beef topside
25 g / 1 oz butter
1 onion, peeled and chopped
100 g / 4oz fresh white
   breadcrumbs
½ teaspoon dried thyme
2 tablespoons chopped fresh
   parsley
salt and pepper
2 teaspoons lemon juice
1 egg, beaten
12 fresh apricots, skinned and
   stoned
3 green dessert apples, cored and
   cut into eighths
4 bay leaves
1 × 375-g / 13-oz can cook-in
   barbecue sauce

Spread the beef flat and cut into 12 strips about 4 cm / 1½ inches wide. Melt the butter and fry the onion for 5 minutes. Remove from the heat, stir in the breadcrumbs, thyme, parsley and salt and pepper to taste. Bind together with the lemon juice and egg. Divide the stuffing equally between the beef strips and roll up.

Thread the stuffed beef rolls on to four skewers, alternating with the apricots, apple slices and bay leaves. Brush with the barbecue sauce.

Place under a preheated moderate grill and cook for 20–25 minutes, turning frequently and basting with the sauce. Serve hot with any remaining barbecue sauce.

Cook's Tip

To stone fresh apricots, halve lengthways along the slight indentation. Turn the halves in opposite directions, then pull them apart and lift out the stone. A 482-g / 1-lb can apricot halves may be used instead.

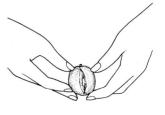

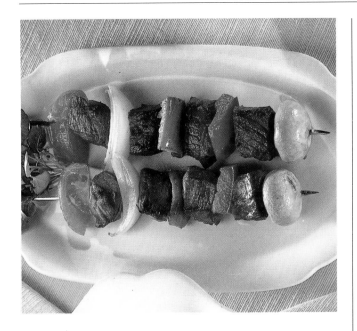

115 | *Beef and Orange Kebabs*

Preparation time
10 minutes

Cooking time
15 minutes

Serves 4

Calories
235 per portion

You will need
*500 g / 1 lb frying steak, cut into
  bite-sized pieces
2–3 tomatoes, quartered
½ green pepper, cored, seeded
  and cut into pieces
½ red pepper, cored, seeded
  and cut into pieces
125 g / 4 oz button mushrooms
1 onion, cut into segments
2 tablespoons oil
grated rind and juice of 1 orange
1 tablespoon soy sauce
pepper
watercress to garnish*

Thread the meat and vegetables alternately on to long skewers, starting with tomato.

Mix together the oil, orange rind and juice, sugar, soy sauce and pepper to taste, and use to coat the kebabs, brushing on with a pastry brush. Cook under a preheated moderate grill, about 7.5 cm / 3 inches away from the heat, for 15 minutes. Brush the kebabs with the oil and orange mixture after 10 minutes and turn over. Garnish with watercress.

Serves with crusty French bread and a green salad.

116 | *Beef and Radish Salad*

Preparation time
15 minutes

Serves 4

Calories
515 per portion

You will need
*1 bunch radishes, with leaves
450 g / 1 lb cold rare roast beef
50 g / 2 oz walnut halves, broken*

For the dressing
*4 tablespoons walnut or olive oil
2 tablespoons orange juice
1 tablespoon wine vinegar
salt and pepper*

Thinly slice the beef and cut into strips about 4 × 1 cm / 1½ × ½ inch and place in a bowl.

Select a few of the best radishes to make 'roses' for garnishing. Thinly slice the remaining radishes and add to the beef with the walnuts.

To make the dressing, mix all the ingredients together and pour over the salad. Toss until well coated.

Arrange in a serving dish. Spoon the beef and radish salad in the centre and garnish with the radish roses and radish leaves.

Cook's Tip

You can substitute boneless chicken or pork for these kebabs. The marinade is suitable for either, but if you use chicken, reduce the cooking time by 1–2 minutes per side.

Cook's Tip

To make radish 'roses', make long cuts from the top of each radish to within 1 cm / ½ inch of the base. Leave in a bowl of iced water or in the refrigerator for several hours until they open out.

117 | Veal Chops with Marjoram Sauce

Preparation time
10 minutes

Cooking time
35 minutes

Serves 4

Calories
289 per portion

You will need
4 large veal chops, about 255 g /
   8 oz each
25 g / 1 oz butter
1 tablespoon oil
1 onion, peeled and finely
   chopped
1 garlic clove, peeled and crushed
3 tablespoons chicken stock
3 tablespoons dry vermouth
1 tablespoon chopped fresh
   marjoram, or 1 teaspoon dried
salt and pepper
4 tablespoons double cream

Heat the butter and oil and fry the chops over moderate heat for 4 minutes on each side. Remove the chops and keep warm.

Fry the onion and garlic for 3 minutes, stirring occasionally, then pour in the stock and vermouth and stir well. Return the chops to the dish and add the marjoram and salt and pepper to taste.

Bring the sauce to the boil, then cover the dish, lower the heat and simmer for 20 minutes.

Increase the heat, bring the sauce to the boil again to reduce the liquid slightly. Add the cream and heat through. Adjust the seasoning if necessary and serve.

Cook's Tip

You are more likely to get veal chops from a butcher than at a supermarket. These meaty chops are very popular in Italy.

118 | Veal Scallopini Mirabeau

Preparation time
20 minutes, plus
chilling

Cooking time
10 minutes

Serves 4

Calories
501 per portion

You will need
2 veal cutlets, about 275 g / 10 oz
   each, boned
25 g / 1 oz plain flour
1 egg, beaten
75 g / 3 oz fine dry white
   breadcrumbs, sieved
4–6 tablespoons butter
2 tablespoons olive oil
anchovy fillets, drained and each
   cut in half lengthways
stuffed olives, sliced
1 lemon, cut into wedges

Cut each veal cutlet across the grain into two thin slices horizontally. Lay the pieces between two sheets of greaseproof paper and pound until thin. Sprinkle with a little flour.

Place the egg in one shallow dish and the breadcrumbs in another. Dip the veal in the egg, draining carefully, then roll in the breadcrumbs, patting the coating on firmly. Chill for at least 30 minutes.

Heat the butter and olive oil in a frying pan large enough to hold all the veal in a single layer. When the butter is foaming, fry the veal over moderate heat for 3–5 minutes on one side, then turn over and arrange a lattice of anchovy strips on each piece. Place an olive slice in each lattice opening and continue cooking for a further 3–5 minutes, or until the breadcrumbs are crisp and golden and the veal is cooked, but still juicy.

Transfer to a heated serving dish. Serve garnished with lemon wedges.

Cook's Tip

The veal should be pounded thinly but not so thin that the breadcrumb coating is nearly the same thickness as the veal. Lay the slices between two sheets of greaseproof paper and flatten gently with a meat mallet or rolling pin.

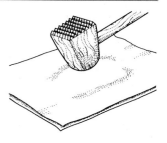

119 | Veal Escalopes with Ham and Cheese

Preparation time
15 minutes

Cooking time
12–15 minutes

Serve 4

Calories
418 per portion

You will need
4 teaspoons plain flour
salt and pepper
4 veal escalopes, about 175 g /
  6 oz each
2 tablespoons olive oil
25 g / 1 oz butter
100 g / 4 oz Parma ham, chopped
2 teaspoons chopped fresh
  marjoram, or ½ teaspoon dried
2 tablespoons Parmesan cheese,
  grated
4 tablespoons Marsala
fresh marjoram or parsley to
  garnish

Place the flour on a plate and season with salt and pepper. Coat the veal escalopes with the flour, shaking off any excess.

Heat the oil and butter and fry the veal quickly on both sides until golden brown.

Divide the ham between the four escalopes and sprinkle with marjoram and cheese. Stir the Marsala into the pan juices and spoon over the veal.

Cover and cook gently for 3–4 minutes until the cheese has melted. Serve hot, garnished with marjoram.

120 | Veal in Lemon Sauce

Preparation time
10 minutes

Cooking time
8–10 minutes

Serves 4

Calories
313 per portion

You will need
2 veal fillets, about 350 g / 12 oz
  each, thinly sliced
4 tablespoons seasoned flour
2 tablespoons olive oil
50 g / 2 oz butter
4 tablespoons lemon juice
4 tablespoons chicken stock or
  water
salt and pepper
chopped fresh parsley and lemon
  slices to garnish

Toss the veal in seasoned flour, shaking off any excess. Heat the oil and half the butter and fry the veal quickly on both sides, for 2–3 minutes, until lightly browned. Remove the veal from the pan and keep warm.

Reduce the heat and stir the lemon juice and stock into the pan, scraping down any sediment. Add salt and pepper to taste. Add the remaining butter to the pan, tilting it until the butter has melted.

Return the veal to the pan and reheat gently. Transfer to a warmed serving dish and sprinkle with chopped parsley. Garnish with lemon slices.

Cook's Tip

Use sage if marjoram isn't available. Both herbs are oftened partnered with veal.

Cook's Tip

When squeezing fresh lemon juice, first roll the lemon on the work surface, pressing firmly. This breaks down the membranes inside and yields more juice.

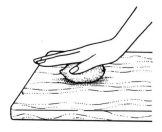

121 | Veal and Mushroom Rolls

Preparation time 10 minutes	**You will need** 4 veal escalopes, about 75 g / 3 oz each
Cooking time 20 minutes	75 g / 3 oz butter 2 rashers back bacon, rinded and cut into 1 cm / ½ inch dice
Serves 4	50 g / 2 oz mushrooms, wiped and finely chopped 2 tablespoons sultanas 1 tablespoon chopped parsley 2 tablespoons grated Cheddar cheese
Calories 449 per portion	2 teaspoons plain flour 175 ml / 6 fl oz dry red wine parsley sprigs to garnish

Flatten the escalopes then cut each one in half.

Melt 25 g / 1 oz of the butter and fry the bacon over moderate heat for 3 minutes, stirring occasionally. Add the mushrooms and cook for a further 2 minutes. Stir in the sultanas, parsley and cheese, then add salt and pepper to taste. Remove from the heat.

Divide the filling between the pieces of veal and press it down well. Roll up the veal and tie each one with string.

Melt the remaining butter and fry the veal rolls over moderate heat for 8 minutes, turning to brown evenly.

Remove the veal from the pan, stir in the flour and pour on the wine. Bring to the boil, and add salt and pepper to taste. Return the veal, cover and simmer over low heat for 10 minutes, turning once. Remove the strings and serve garnished with parsley.

Cook's Tip

Rather than grating a small amount of Cheddar cheese every time you need it, as in this recipe, freeze it in a larger quantity. Grated cheese will keep for up to 6 months, and can be used straight from the freezer.

122 | Deep-fried Veal and Vegetables

Preparation time 25 minutes, plus chilling	**You will need** 50 g / 2 oz plain flour salt and pepper 4 eggs, beaten
Cooking time 12–15 minutes	350 g / 12 oz dried white breadcrumbs 350 g / 12 oz escalope of veal, cut into 2.5 cm / 1 inch wide strips
Serves 4	2 small aubergines, thinly sliced 2 small courgettes, cut into matchstick strips
Calories 224 per portion	225 g / 8 oz mushrooms, wiped 8 artichoke hearts, drained if canned oil for deep-frying lemon wedges to garnish

Place the seasoned flour in a polythene bag with salt and pepper. Place the breadcrumbs and eggs in separate bowls.

Toss the meat and vegetables, including the artichoke hearts, in seasoned flour, shaking off any excess. Dip in beaten egg, then coat with breadcrumbs. Chill for 30 minutes to set the coating.

Heat the oil to 180–190C / 350–375F or until a cube of bread browns in 30 seconds.

Fry the meat and vegetables, a few at a time, for 3 minutes until crisp and golden brown. Drain on paper towels and keep warm while you fry the remainder. Serve hot, garnished with lemon wedges.

Cook's Tip

To make dried breadcrumbs, spread fresh breadcrumbs over a baking sheet and dry out in a 150C / 300F / Gas 2 oven for 30 minutes.

123 | *Veal in Red Gravy*

Preparation time
6 minutes

Cooking time
4 minutes

Serves 4

Calories
140 per portion

You will need
1 tablespoon oil
1 small onion, peeled and finely
   chopped
1 garlic clove, peeled and crushed
2.5 cm / 1 inch piece root ginger,
   very finely chopped
3 veal escalopes, about 75 g /3 oz
   each, cut into matchstick strips
1 tablespoon tomato purée
1 tablespoon soy sauce
salt and pepper
1 tablespoon sweet sherry
3 tablespoons water
1 teaspoon sugar (optional)
spring onion strips to garnish

Heat the oil and fry the onion gently for 30 seconds. Add the garlic and ginger and stir-fry for 30 seconds. Push the mixture to one side of the pan and tilt the pan to let the juices run out over the base.

Add the veal and increase the heat. Cook, stirring, for 2 minutes, until the veal is evenly coloured.

Lower the heat and stir in the remaining ingredients, adding sugar to taste if liked. Cook, stirring, for 30 seconds. Serve at once, garnished with spring onion strips.

124 | *Frikadeller*

Preparation time
15 minutes

Cooking time
15–20 minutes

Serves 4

Calories
381 per portion

You will need
225 g / 8 oz minced veal
225 g / 8 oz minced pork
1 small onion, peeled and grated
25 g / 1 oz plain flour
1 teaspoon dried dill weed
salt and pepper
1 egg, beaten
300 ml / ½ pint milk
25 g / 1 oz butter
2 tablespoons oil
lemon slices to garnish

Mix together the veal, pork, onion, flour, dill and salt and pepper to taste.

Beat in the egg, then gradually add the milk, beating well until the mixture is fluffy.

Melt the butter and oil together in a large frying pan.

Shape the meat mixture into oblongs with the help of two tablespoons. Drop into the pan and cook gently for 15–20 minutes, turning frequently, until brown on all sides.

Garnish with lemon slices and serve at once.

Cook's Tip

Have all the ingredients ready before starting to stir-fry. The cooking time is fast, so it is important to finely cut the onion and root ginger. If the pieces are too thick they will still taste raw when the cooking is finished.

Cook's Tip

These minced meat patties are the national dish of Denmark. Other meats are sometimes used but veal and pork is the traditional combination. Popular accompaniments are pickled beetroot and cucumbers.

125 | Prune-Stuffed Fillet of Pork

Preparation time
15 minutes

Cooking time
30 minutes

Serves 4

Calories
300 per portion

You will need
2 pork fillets or tenderloin, about 350 g / 12 oz each, well trimmed
8 prunes, halved and stoned
2 tablespoons seedless raisins
3 tablespoons clear honey
1 tablespoon butter
1 teaspoon plain flour
150 ml / ¼ pint sweet cider
salt and pepper

Cut the pork fillets lengthways without cutting them right through.

Arrange the prune halves along one side of each fillet, cover the prunes with 1 tablespoon of the raisins and with 1 tablespoon of the honey. Close up the fillets again, enclosing the fruit, and tie with thin string.

Melt the butter and fry the pork fillets until brown on both sides.

Stir in the flour, pour on the cider and bring to the boil. Add salt and pepper to taste, and the remaining raisins. Simmer, covered, turning the pork once, for 25 minutes until cooked through.

Remove the string and spread the remaining honey along the fillets of pork. Glaze under a preheated hot grill for 2 minutes.

126 | Pork Fillet with Orange and Ginger

Preparation time
15 minutes

Cooking time
10–12 minutes

Serves 4

Calories
221 per portion

You will need
25 g / 1 oz butter
450 g / l lb pork fillet or tenderloin, sliced into 5 mm / ¼ inch rounds or medallions
salt and pepper
1 tablespoon ginger marmalade
1 tablespoon brown sugar
1 tablespoon orange juice
1 tablespoon cider vinegar
4 spring onions, finely shredded

For the garnish
matchstick strips of orange rind
mint sprigs

Melt the butter and quickly brown the pork on all sides for 6–8 minutes until golden and tender. Season with salt and pepper to taste. Remove with a slotted spoon and arrange decoratively on a warmed serving plate. Keep warm.

Add the marmalade, sugar, orange juice, cider vinegar and spring onions to the pan juices and heat until the mixture forms a syrupy glaze. Spoon over the meat.

Garnish with orange rind and mint.

Cook's Tip

Orange juice is a good alternative to the cider in this recipe. You can also add the finely grated rind of 1 orange.

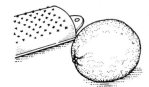

Cook's Tip

For a dinner party, serve this quick but impressive looking dish with boiled rice and a green vegetable such as French beans. Because the sauce is so rich and flavourful the accompanying vegetables should be kept simple.

127 | Pork with Herbs and Apple

Preparation time
6 minutes

Cooking time
10 minutes

Serves 4

Calories
142 per portion

You will need
1 tablespoon oil
1 onion, peeled and finely chopped
1 cooking apple, peeled and coarsely grated
2–3 pork fillets, about 750 g / 1½ lb, thinly sliced
1 teaspoon dried sage
1 tablespoon chopped fresh parsley
1 teaspoon soft brown sugar
1 tablespoon soy sauce blended with 1 teaspoon cornflour
150 ml / ¼ pint vegetable stock

Heat the oil and fry the onion and apple for 4–5 minutes until soft. Push to one side of the pan and tilt the pan to let the juices run out over the base.

Increase the heat, add the pork and herbs to the pan and stir-fry for 2–3 minutes until the pork is evenly coloured. Sprinkle in the sugar and blended soy sauce. Lower the heat, add the vegetable stock and cook gently, stirring, until thickened; do not boil. Serve at once with a green vegetable such as broccoli.

128 | Pork with Orange Sauce

Preparation time
8 minutes

Cooking time
10 minutes

Serves 4–6

Calories
162 per portion

You will need
4–6 pork chops, about 150 g / 5 oz each, boned and trimmed into neat ovals
1 tablespoon cornflour blended with 2 tablespoons water
1 teaspoon soft brown sugar
finely grated rind of 1 orange
juice of 2 oranges
2 teaspoons oil
1 teaspoon finely chopped ginger
salt and pepper
watercress sprigs to garnish

Cook the pork under a preheated moderate grill for 5 minutes on each side or until cooked through.

Meanwhile, place the blended cornflour, sugar, orange rind and juice in a bowl and stir well.

Heat the oil and fry the ginger for 30 seconds, stirring. Pour in the orange mixture and cook, stirring, for 1½–2 minutes until thickened. Season with salt and pepper to taste.

Arrange the pork on warmed plates and spoon the sauce over part of it and on to the plate. Serve at once, garnished with watercress.

Cook's Tip

Pork fillet, or tenderloin, is a very lean cut. It should be a pale colour with tinges of pink when you buy it. Although expensive, it is not wasteful as it doesn't contain any bones or fat.

Cook's Tip

Instead of pork chops, you can use thick slices of pork fillet or tenderloin. Because these do not contain extra fat, it may be necessary to brush them with oil once or twice during cooking so the outside does not become charred before the inside is thoroughly cooked.

129 | Pork Chops with Spicy Mustard Cream

Preparation time
5 minutes

Cooking time
35–40 minutes

Serves 4

Calories
353 per portion

You will need
1 tablespoon oil
4 pork chops, about 175 g / 6 oz each
4 tablespoons whole grain mustard
1 teaspoon grated nutmeg
300 ml / ½ pint dry white wine
salt and pepper
150 ml / ¼ pint double cream
1 tablespoon chopped fresh parsley to garnish

Heat the oil in a deep frying pan with a lid. Score the fat on the pork chops, and brown them quickly on either side. Remove and keep warm.

Add the mustard, nutmeg, wine and salt and pepper to taste, blending well. Return the chops to the pan, cover and simmer gently for 20 minutes until the chops are cooked through.

Add the cream and cook gently until the sauce reduces and thickens. Garnish with chopped parsley. Serve with freshly cooked green noodles and a crisp salad.

Cook's Tip

Instead of using dry white wine, the pork chops can be cooked in a sauce made with chicken stock. If you use a stock cube, do not add too much salt to the sauce because the cubes are very salty.

130 | Pork with Prune Sauce

Preparation time
8 minutes

Cooking time
20 minutes

Serves 4–6

Calories
339 per portion

You will need
4–6 pork loin chops, about 150 g / 5 oz each
1 tablespoon oil
1 small onion, peeled and thinly sliced
1 garlic clove, peeled and crushed
1 × 425-g / 15-oz can unsweetened prunes
2 teaspoons cornflour
1 tablespoon soy sauce
2 teaspoons wine vinegar
brown sugar
watercress sprigs to garnish

Cook the pork chops under a preheated moderate grill for 10 minutes on each side or until cooked through.

Meanwhile, heat the oil and fry the onion for 2 minutes, stirring. Stir in the garlic and set aside.

Drain the prunes, reserving the juice. Remove and discard the stones. Set aside 4–6 for garnishing and place the remaining prunes and the juice in a liquidizer or food processor with the cornflour, soy sauce, vinegar and onion mixture and purée. Pour into the pan and cook, stirring, until thick and shiny. Stir in sugar to taste.

Divide the sauce between individual warmed serving plates and top each with a pork chop. Serve at once, garnished with the reserved prunes and watercress sprigs.

Cook's Tip

Grilling is one of the healthiest ways to cook pork because it allows the excess fat to drip off. For successful grilling, preheat the grill so it is hot, and have the meat at room temperature.

131 | *Pork Fillet in Egg and Lemon Sauce*

Preparation time
15 minutes

Cooking time
20 minutes

Serves 4

Calories
521 per portion

You will need
*2 pork fillets, about 350 g / 12 oz
    each, trimmed
1 tablespoon oil
75 g / 3 oz butter
100 g / 4 oz button mushrooms,
    wiped and thinly sliced
2 tablespoons plain flour
300 ml / ½ pint chicken stock
2 eggs
2 tablespoons lemon juice
1 tablespoon water
1 tablespoon chopped fresh
    parsley to garnish*

Cut the pork into 2 cm / ¾ inch thick slices. Heat the oil with 25 g / 1 oz of the butter and fry the pork over moderate heat for 4 minutes on each side. Add half the remaining butter and the mushrooms and cook for a further 4 minutes, turning the meat once. Remove the meat and mushrooms and keep them warm.

To make the sauce, melt the remaining butter, stir in the flour and cook for 2 minutes. Gradually stir in the stock, until the sauce boils. Beat the eggs until they are frothy, then beat in the lemon juice and add the water. Reduce the heat.

Add 5 tablespoons of the hot stock to the egg mixture, then pour it into the sauce remaining in the pan. Stir until the sauce thickens, and add salt and pepper to taste.

Add the pork and mushrooms to the sauce and serve at once, garnished with parsley.

Cook's Tip

After adding the eggs to the sauce, do not boil or the eggs will scramble.

132 | *Pork and Mango Curry*

Preparation time
15 minutes

Cooking time
30 minutes

Serves 4–6

Calories
601 per portion

You will need
*750 g / 1½ lb pork fillet, cut into
    2.5 cm / 1 inch cubes
25 g / 1 oz plain flour
2 tablespoons oil
1 Spanish onion, peeled and sliced
2 small green or red peppers,
    cored, seeded and sliced
1 teaspoon tumeric
2 teaspoons salt
1 tablespoon curry powder
1 teaspoon ground cumin
1 teaspoon ground ginger
½ teaspoon chilli seasoning
5 tomatoes, peeled and chopped
2 teaspoons tomato purée
450 ml / ¾ pint light meat stock
750 g / 1½ lb small new potatoes,
    scrubbed or peeled
2 large mangos, peeled, stoned
    and sliced*

Toss the pork in the flour to coat. Heat the oil and fry the pork for 5 minutes until golden. Add the onion and peppers and cook for a further 3 minutes. Add the tumeric, salt, curry powder, cumin, ginger and chilli seasoning and cook for 1 minute, stirring constantly.

Add the tomatoes, tomato purée and stock, blending well. Add the potatoes, cover and cook for 15 minutes over a gentle heat, stirring occasionally. Add the mango slices and cook for a further 5 minutes until the potatoes are tender. Serve at once.

Cook's Tip

Some ideal accompaniments to serve with the spicy curry are boiled rice, banana slices tossed in lemon juice, mango chutney and chopped cucumber in plain unsweetened yogurt.

133 | *Bacon Steaks with Cucumber Sauce*

Preparation time
5 minutes

Cooking time
8–9 minutes

Serves 4

Calories
269 per portion

You will need
4 bacon steaks, about 100 g / 4 oz
   each, fat snipped
1 teaspoon oil
cucumber slices to garnish

For the sauce
1 cucumber, peeled and sliced
salt
20 g / ¾ oz butter
20 g / ¾ oz plain flour
300 ml / ½ pint milk
2 tablespoons double cream
1 tablespoon chopped chives
pepper
pinch cayenne pepper

Brush the bacon steaks with oil and cook them under a preheated moderate grill for 4–5 minutes on each side.

Meanwhile, to make the sauce, cook the cucumber in boiling, salted water for 3 minutes, then drain thoroughly and dry. Melt the butter, stir in the flour and stir over moderate heat for 30 seconds. Gradually pour on the milk, stirring constantly, until boiling, then simmer for 3 minutes. Stir the cucumber, cream and chives into the sauce, and add salt, pepper and cayenne to taste.

Spoon a little of the sauce on to the bacon steaks and serve the rest separately. Garnish with cucumber slices.

134 | *Grilled Gammon with Orange Butter*

Preparation time
10 minutes, plus chilling

Cooking time
10 minutes

Serves 4

Calories
856 per portion

You will need
4 gammon steaks, about 150 g / 6
   oz each
65 g / 2½ oz butter, melted
fresh parsley springs to garnish

For the seasoned butter
2 oranges
100 g / 4 oz butter
2 teaspoons finely chopped
   parsley

To make the seasoned butter, finely grate the rind from the oranges. Mix this with the butter, then form into a neat, long log. Roll in the parsley, then wrap in cling film and chill until ready to serve.

Snip the fat on the steaks at 2.5 cm / 1 inch intervals. Cook under a preheated grill, brushing with the butter, for 5 minutes on each side.

Meanwhile, peel the oranges and thinly slice. Cut the butter into four portions.

Serve the gammon steaks, topped with the butter and garnished with the orange slices.

Cook's Tip

Snipping the fat around the bacon steaks at 2.5 cm / 1 inch intervals prevents the edges from curling up during cooking.

Cook's Tip

Flavoured butters are ideal to serve with most grilled meats. They freeze well, so it's easy to have a selection on hand. Try finely chopped mixed herbs with steaks and mint with lamb chops.

135 | Lamb with Chilled Cucumber Sauce

Preparation time
10 minutes

Cooking time
10 minutes

Serves 4

Calories
517 per portion

You will need
8 noisettes of lamb
8 slices bread, crusts removed
40 g / 1½ oz butter

For the sauce
½ cucumber, peeled and grated
150 ml / ¼ pint unsweetened plain
  yogurt
½ tablespoon chopped fresh mint
salt and pepper

To make the sauce, mix together all the ingredients. Cover and chill until ready to serve.

Cook the noisettes under a preheated hot grill for 2–3 minutes on either side, then about 7 minutes on a lower setting until done to desired taste.

Meanwhile, cut the bread into rounds with a biscuit cutter. Melt the butter, then fry the bread until golden on each side. Drain well on paper towels and sprinkle with salt.

To serve, place two fried bread rounds on each plate and top with noisettes. Serve hot with the chilled sauce.

136 | Noisettes Niçoise

Preparation time
10 minutes

Cooking time
10 minutes

Serves 4

Calories
290 per portion

You will need
8 noisettes of lamb
2 onions, peeled and finely
  chopped
2 garlic cloves, peeled and finely
  chopped
4 tomatoes, skinned and chopped
1 tablespoon oil
salt and pepper
8 black olives

Cook the noisettes under a preheated hot grill for 2–3 minutes on either side, then 7 minutes on a lower setting until done to desired taste.

Meanwhile, heat the oil and fry the onions and garlic for 5 minutes until tender. Add the tomatoes and salt and pepper to taste. Continue cooking until the tomatoes are heated through and tender.

Transfer the noisettes to a heated serving dish and spoon over the tomato mixture. Add the olives and serve at once.

Cook's Tip

This refreshing sauce, also called raita, is often served as a cooling accompaniment with hot, spicy curries. If you have time, sprinkle the grated cucumber with salt and leave for 30 minutes for all excess liquid to drain off. If time is short, put the cucumber in a sieve and squeeze out as much liquid as possible with the back of a wooden spoon.

Cook's Tip

You can ask your butcher to make the noisettes or do it yourself. Remove the bone from loin or best end of neck chops. Roll the meat into a neat round with the fat on the outside. Tie with string.

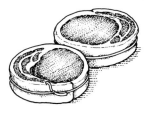

137 | Kiwi Lamb Chops

Preparation time
5 minutes

Cooking time
20 minutes

Serves 4–6

Calories
431 per portion

You will need
4–6 lamb chump chops, about
175 g / 6 oz each, cut in half
1 kiwi fruit, sliced, to garnish

For the sauce
3–4 kiwi fruit, sliced
sugar to taste

Grill the lamb chops under a preheated moderate grill for 10 minutes on each side.

Stew the kiwi fruit in a little water until it can be mashed with a fork, then add sugar to taste, keeping the sauce sharp.

Arrange the lamb on a warmed serving dish and garnish with kiwi fruit slices. Serve immediately with the sauce spooned over.

138 | Lamb Chops in Red Wine Sauce

Preparation time
15 minutes

Cooking time
30 minutes

Oven temperature
190C, 375F, Gas 5

Serves 4

Calories
350 per portion

You will need
4 loin of lamb chops, about 100g /
4 oz each, well trimmed
1 garlic clove, peeled and finely
chopped
25 g / 1 oz butter
2 small courgettes, sliced
175 g / 6 oz button mushrooms,
sliced
4 large tomatoes, skinned and
sliced
1 tablespoon clear honey
150 ml / ¼ pint dry red wine
1 tablespoon chopped fresh
marjoram, or 1 teaspoon dried
salt and pepper
1 tablespoon chopped fresh
parsley to garnish

Fry the chops with the garlic over moderate heat for 3 minutes on each side. Transfer the chops to a casserole, discarding any fat remaining in the pan.

Melt the butter and fry the courgettes and mushrooms, stirring once or twice, for 2 minutes. Add to the chops with the tomatoes, honey, wine, marjoram and salt and pepper to taste.

Cover the casserole and cook in a preheated oven for 15–20 minutes until the chops are cooked to your liking.

Serve garnished with parsley.

Cook's Tip

For extra tender chops, gently rub all sides with a kiwi fruit and set aside for 30 minutes before grilling. The kiwi fruit contains an enzyme which is a natural meat tenderizer.

Cook's Tip

The casserole can be made a day ahead. Set aside to cool completely, then cover and store in the refrigerator. Reheat thoroughly before serving.

139 | Lamb with Rosemary

Preparation time
6 minutes

Cooking time
10 minutes

Serves 4

Calories
189 per portion

You will need
2 teaspoons oil
1 onion, peeled and finely
 chopped
2 garlic cloves, peeled and
 crushed
2–3 large lamb chump chops,
 trimmed and cubed
2 teaspoons soy sauce
1 sprig fresh rosemary, finely
 chopped, or 1 teaspoon dried
2 teaspoons cornflour blended
 with 3 tablespoons water
150 ml / ¼ pint hot lamb stock or
 water

Heat the oil and stir-fry the onion for 2 minutes, then stir in the garlic. Push the mixture to one side of the pan and add the meat. Stir-fry for 3–4 minutes until evenly browned. Push to one side and tilt the pan so the fat runs out of the meat. Drain off this excess fat.

Mix the meat with the onions and move back into the centre of the pan. Add the soy sauce and the rosemary and stir-fry for a few seconds. Transfer to warmed serving plates using a slotted spoon and keep warm.

Pour the blended cornflour into the pan and stir to release any pan juices. Add the stock and simmer, stirring, until thickened.

Spoon the thickened sauce over the meat. Serve at once, garnished with rosemary.

140 | Greek Cinnamon Lamb

Preparation time
10 minutes, plus chilling

Cooking time
7–8 minutes

Serves 4
as a starter

Calories
390 per portion

You will need
125 g / 4 oz Greek yogurt
2 tablespoons olive oil
2 tablespoons chopped fresh mint
1 garlic clove, peeled and crushed
2 tablespoons honey
¼ teaspoon ground cinnamon
salt and pepper
450 g / 1 lb lamb neck fillet,
 trimmed and cut into small
 cubes
8 bay leaves
lemon wedges to garnish

Mix together the yogurt, oil, mint, garlic, honey, cinnamon and salt and pepper to taste, blending well. Add the lamb and stir to coat. Cover and chill for 4 hours.

Drain the lamb from the marinade with a slotted spoon and thread on to four small skewers with the bay leaves.

Cook under a preheated hot grill or over glowing coals on a barbecue for 7–8 minutes, basting frequently with the marinade, until cooked through.

Serve hot garnished with lemon wedges and with any remaining marinade drizzled over.

Cook's Tip

Cornflour is the thickening agent in the sauce. Be sure to taste the sauce before taking it off the heat and spooning over the sauce. The cornflour needs sufficient cooking so it doesn't taste raw.

Cook's Tip

Do not substitute dried mint for fresh in this recipe. If fresh mint isn't available, use another fresh herb such as coriander or parsley. The finely grated rind of a large orange is another suitable alternative.

141 | Liver with Orange

Preparation time
6 minutes

Cooking time
7 minutes

Serves 4

Calories
201 per portion

You will need
350 g / 12 oz lambs' or calves'
    liver, cut into small pieces
1 tablespoon cornflour
1 tablespoon oil
finely grated rind and juice of 1
    orange
2 teaspoons soy sauce
4–5 tablespoons water
salt and pepper
2 oranges, peeled and sliced
watercress sprigs to garnish

Coat the liver in the cornflour, shaking off any excess. Heat the oil and stir-fry the liver for 4 minutes until evenly browned. Add the orange rind and juice, soy sauce and water, then stir well and add the salt and pepper to taste and orange slices. Heat through gently, without boiling.

Transfer to a warmed serving dish and garnish with watercress sprigs. Serve at once.

142 | Crispy-coated Liver

Preparation time
10 minutes, plus chilling

Cooking time
15 minutes

Serves 4

Calories
504 per portion

You will need
75 g / 3 oz butter
1 large onion, peeled and sliced
    into rings
25 g / 1 oz plain flour
salt and pepper
½ teaspoon mixed dried herbs
1 egg
1 tablespoon milk
450 g / 1 lb lambs' liver, thinly
    sliced
50 g / 2 oz rolled porridge oats
125 ml / 4 fl oz dry sherry
125 ml / 4 fl oz chicken stock

Melt 25 g / 1 oz of the butter and fry the onion rings over moderate heat for 5–6 minutes, turning occasionally. Remove from the pan and keep warm.

Season the flour with salt, pepper and herbs and put on a plate. Beat the egg and milk together in a shallow bowl.

Dip the liver slices in the seasoned flour then dip into the egg and milk and roll in the oats. Press the oats firmly to make an even coating. Chill for 30 minutes.

Melt the remaining butter and when the foaming has subsided, fry the liver over moderate heat for 3 minutes on each side, until the coating is crisp and brown.

Remove from the pan and keep warm. Tip in any remaining flour and stir well. Pour on the sherry and stock, then bring to the boil, stirring, and season to taste.

Arrange the liver on a heated serving dish, scatter the onion rings on top and pour over the sauce.

Cook's Tip

To quickly coat the liver with the cornflour without any mess, put the meat in a polythene bag with the cornflour and shake. If you try to do it on a plate, the coating may be too thick and you may not have sufficient cornflour.

Cook's Tip

To tenderise liver you can cover with milk and leave to marinate for an hour or so. Drain and pat dry before cooking.

143 | Calves' Liver with Sage Sauce

Preparation time
20 minutes

Cooking time
20 minutes

Serves 6

Calories
340 per portion

You will need
75 g / 3 oz butter
1 tablespoon oil
6 slices calves' liver, 90–100g /
    3½–4 oz each
1 onion, peeled and chopped
75 g / 3 oz button mushrooms,
    wiped and sliced
1 tablespoon plain flour
300 ml / ½ pint beef stock
150 ml / ¼ pint dry red wine
1 tablespoon chopped fresh sage
    or 1 teaspoon dried
salt and pepper
sprigs of fresh sage leaves to
    garnish (optional)

Melt the butter and oil and fry the liver quickly on either side until it is light golden brown. Remove from the pan and keep warm.

Fry the onion in the pan juices for 3–4 minutes, then add the mushrooms and cook for a further 3–4 minutes. Remove the pan from the heat.

Sprinkle in the flour and mix gently, taking care not to break up the mushrooms. Return the pan to the heat and gradually add the stock and wine with the sage and salt and pepper to taste.

Return the liver to the pan and coat with the sauce. Simmer gently for 8–10 minutes. Arrange the liver slices overlapping on a serving dish, pour over the sauce and garnish with the fresh sage leaves if liked.

Cook's Tip

Ask your butcher to slice the liver as thinly as possible. That way it cooks quickly and remains very tender.

144 | Japanese-style Kidneys

Preparation time
25 minutes, plus
marinating

Cooking time
10–12 minutes

Serves 4

Calories
415 per portion

You will need
4 tablespoons soy sauce
3 tablespoons dry sherry
2 tablespoons clear honey
300-ml / ½-pint beef consommé
1 garlic clove, peeled and crushed
pinch five spice powder
12 lamb's kidneys, halved and
    cored
25 g / 1 oz seasoned plain flour
40 g / 1½ oz butter
1 tablespoon cornflour
salt and pepper
spring onion curls and carrot
    shapes to garnish

Mix the soy sauce, sherry, honey, beef consommé, garlic and five spice powder in a bowl. Add the kidneys, tossing well to coat, cover and marinate for 30 minutes.

Remove the kidneys and pat dry with paper towels. Toss in seasoned flour to coat. Melt the butter and fry the kidneys over a moderate heat for 5 minutes, turning occasionally. Remove with a slotted spoon and reserve.

Add the marinade to the pan and bring to the boil. Blend the cornflour with a little water and pour into the sauce, stirring constantly, until lightly thickened.

Add the kidneys to the sauce with salt and pepper to taste. Cook for 1–2 minutes or until the kidneys are heated through and cooked but still tender. Garnish with spring onion curls and carrot scrolls or decorative shapes and serve with hot rice if liked.

Cook's Tip

To make carrot and other vegetable shapes, slice a peeled carrot, swede or turnip crossways and cut out shapes with a canapé cutter or knife. Traditional shapes include hearts, fish, moons and flowers.

Vegetables

Lightly cooked, tasty vegetables can be the highlight of any meal. With the recipes in this chapter you can take advantage of seasonal produce and introduce new variety in your meals. To preserve as many nutrients as possible, prepare vegetables just before cooking and serve them pleasingly firm for maximum flavour and colour.

145 | Asparagus with Lemon Butter

Preparation time
12 minutes

Cooking time
20–30 minutes

Serves 4

Calories
337 per portion

You will need
1 kg / 2 lb asparagus
salt

For the butter
175 g / 6 oz butter
finely grated rind of 1 large lemon

Trim the asparagus, cutting away the woody part of the stalks and paring the stalk with a vegetable peeler if it is tough.

Tie the stalks into four bundles. Stand upright in the tallest pan you have. Pour in boiling water to come as far up the bundles as possible, then cover the tips of the asparagus with foil. Simmer until tender: 20 minutes for thin spears and 25–30 minutes for thicker spears.

Meanwhile, melt the butter and stir in the lemon rind. Keep warm.

To serve, drain the asparagus bundles, untie and place on a warmed serving dish. Either pour the melted butter over or serve it separately for spooning over the individual portions.

146 | Marinated Artichoke Hearts

Preparation time
10 minutes, plus standing

Serves 4

Calories
170 per portion

You will need
4 medium-size artichoke hearts, cooked
50 g / 2 oz button mushrooms, thinly sliced
4 tablespoons French dressing
1 tablespoon chopped fresh parsley or chives
100 g / 4 oz streaky bacon, rinded

Put the artichoke hearts and mushrooms in a large bowl.

Mix the French dressing with the herbs and pour over. Stir well, then leave to marinate for 10 minutes.

Meanwhile, grill the bacon until crisp. Drain and leave to cool.

Just before serving, chop the bacon, add it to the salad and toss well. Arrange on individual serving plates and serve at once.

Cook's Tip

When buying asparagus, the buds should be tight and the spears fresh looking with a good colour. Avoid any that are dirty and wrinkled. It's best to cook them on the day of purchase.

Cook's Tip

To save time just before serving, marinate the artichoke hearts and mushrooms in the French dressing and parsley (or chives) for several hours. Cover with cling film and refrigerate until 15 minutes before serving, then bring back to room temperature before serving.

147 | *Chilled French Beans*

Preparation time
10 minutes

Cooking time
5 minutes

Serves 4

Calories
98 per portion

You will need
450 g /1 lb French beans, topped and tailed
salt

For the dressing
6 tablespoons olive oil
grated rind of 1 small lemon
2 tablespoons lemon juice
1 small garlic clove, peeled and crushed
2 hard-boiled eggs, shelled and finely chopped
8 small black olives
pepper

Put the beans into a pan with a little salt. Just cover with boiling water and simmer for about 5 minutes until cooked, but not limp and soft.

Drain the beans and rinse under cold water.

To make the dressing, pour the olive oil into a bowl large enough to hold the beans. Add the lemon rind, lemon juice, garlic, eggs, olives and salt and pepper and mix well.

Add the beans to the dressing and toss until well coated. This goes well with cold chicken, meat or fish.

148 | *Broad Beans with Sesame Seeds*

Preparation time
5 minutes for frozen beans, 15 minutes for fresh beans

Cooking time
10–15 minutes

Serves 4

Calories
216 per portion

You will need
450 g / 1 lb broad beans, fresh or frozen
2 tablespoons sesame seeds
25 g / 1 oz butter
1 tablespoon lemon juice
pepper

Cook the beans in boiling salted water for 5–15 minutes, depending on whether fresh or frozen, until tender.

Meanwhile, toast the sesame seeds under a moderate grill to brown them evenly.

Drain the beans. Put the butter in the pan and melt. When just beginning to brown, add the lemon juice and pepper to taste.

Tip the beans back into the pan and toss well in the butter. Serve, sprinkled with the sesame seeds.

Cook's Tip

Rinsing the beans under cold water is done for two reasons. It stops the beans cooking so they remain crisp yet tender, and it also 'sets' the bright green colour. The salad may be assembled several hours in advance, covered and chilled.

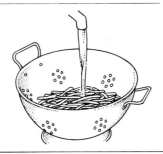

Cook's Tip

When the sesame seeds are toasted enough they will start to pop.

149 | *Broccoli Cheese*

Preparation time
5 minutes

Cooking time
10 minutes

Serves 4

Calories
150 per portion

You will need
1 tablespoon oil
1 onion, peeled and finely
    chopped
4 tablespoons water
450 g / 1 lb broccoli, stems
    chopped and florets left whole
1 tablespoon soy sauce

For the sauce
1 teaspoon whole grain mustard
2 level teaspoons cornflour
    blended with 3 tablespoons
    cold water
600 ml / 1 pint milk
3 tablespoons finely grated
    Parmesan cheese

To make the sauce, stir the mustard into the blended cornflour until smooth, then stir into the milk. Bring to the boil, stirring, then simmer, still stirring, for 2 minutes until thickened. Remove from the heat, sprinkle in the cheese and stir until melted. Set aside.

Heat the oil and fry the onion for 2 minutes without browning. Add the water and broccoli and cook, stirring and turning the vegetables over with two large spoons, for 5–6 minutes until the broccoli is tender, but still crisp. Stir in the soy sauce and transfer to warmed serving plates using a slotted spoon.

Add any gravy left in the pan to the cheese sauce and reheat gently. Spoon over the vegetables. Serve at once.

150 | *Cold Broccoli with Yogurt*

Preparation time
10 minutes, plus
cooling

Cooking time
15 minutes

Serves 4
as a starter

Calories
113 per portion

You will need
750 g / 1½ lb broccoli spears
salt and pepper
150 ml / ¼ pint plain yogurt
1 teaspoon olive oil
1 teaspoon lemon juice
50 g / 2 oz button mushrooms,
    wiped and thinly sliced
1 tablespoon walnut halves

Cut the broccoli into even-sized pieces, about 2.5 cm / 1 inch in length. Cook in boiling salted water until just tender. Drain and cool.

Mix together the yogurt, oil, lemon juice, salt and pepper to taste.

Toss together the broccoli and mushrooms and pour on the yogurt mixture. Toss lightly and garnish with the walnuts. Leave to stand at room temperature for at least 20 minutes before serving.

Cook's Tip

The sauce is removed from the heat before the cheese is added so the fat doesn't run out of the cheese and make the sauce greasy. Do not boil the sauce when reheating or the same thing may happen.

Cook's Tip

After draining the broccoli, quickly rinse under cold water. This stops the cooking so the pieces are tender yet still remain crisp.

151 | Okra and Mushrooms with Sunflower Seeds

Preparation time
15 minutes

Cooking time
15–20 minutes

Serves 4

Calories
139 per portion

You will need
2 teaspoons oil
2 tablespoons sunflower seeds
25 g / 1 oz butter
350 g / 12 oz okra, topped and tailed
100 g / 4 oz button mushrooms, wiped and halved
salt and pepper

Heat the oil in a small pan and cook the sunflower seeds for a minute or two until brown. Drain on paper towels and set aside.

Melt the butter in a frying pan or wok and stir-fry the okra quickly for 3–4 minutes. Add the mushrooms and stir-fry for a further 3–4 minutes.

Sprinkle with salt and pepper to taste. Cover the pan and leave to cook for 10 minutes, until the mushrooms are soft and the okra tender but still crisp.

Uncover and cook quickly for a minute or two to reduce the liquid in the pan. Spoon into a warmed dish and sprinkle with the sunflower seeds. Serve at once.

152 | Button Mushrooms with Peppercorns

Preparation time
10 minutes

Cooking time
15 minutes

Serves 4

Calories
270 per portion

You will need
1 tablespoon olive oil
450 g / 1 lb small button mushrooms, wiped and halved
4 tablespoons water
salt
4 slices wholemeal bread, crusts removed
2 tablespoons oil
25 g / 1 oz butter
3 teaspoons green peppercorns, well drained and lightly crushed
2 tablespoons double or whipping cream
coriander leaves or parsley sprigs to garnish

Heat the oil and fry the mushrooms for 5 minutes until just beginning to brown.

Add the water and a little salt, cover and simmer for 10 minutes.

Meanwhile, cut the bread slices into 1 cm / ½ inch dice. Heat the oil and butter until sizzling, then add the bread and fry until golden brown. Drain well on paper towels.

Stir the peppercorns and cream into the mushrooms and reheat gently without boiling. Tip into a warm serving dish and scatter with the croûtons. Serve immediately, garnished with coriander.

Cook's Tip

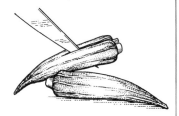

Okra, also known as ladies' fingers, contains a natural thickening agent which it releases during cooking. It is a traditional ingredient in many Caribbean dishes. Large pods can be halved lengthways.

Cook's Tip

Green peppercorns are much softer than the traditional dried black peppercorns, so they can easily be crushed. They are sold in small jars or tins and must be drained before use.

153 | Crisp-topped Mushrooms

Preparation time
6 minutes

Cooking time
12 minutes

Serves 4

Calories
192 per portion

You will need
2 tablespoons oil
450 g / 1 lb small mushrooms, wiped
1 onion, peeled and finely chopped
2 small garlic cloves, peeled and crushed
3 slices wholemeal bread, crusts removed and made into crumbs
2 slices lean cooked ham, diced
1 tablespoon chopped fresh parsley
salt and pepper
about 2 tablespoons grated Parmesan cheese
watercress sprigs and mushroom slices to garnish

Heat half the oil and gently fry the mushrooms for 4–5 minutes. Transfer to a flameproof dish and keep warm.

Heat the remaining oil and stir-fry the onion for 2–3 minutes. Stir in the garlic, breadcrumbs, ham, parsley and salt and pepper to taste and mix well. Spoon over the mushrooms.

Sprinkle with the Parmesan cheese and place under a preheated hot grill until the cheese has melted and the topping is crisp. Serve hot, garnished with the watercress and mushrooms.

154 | Baked Garlic and Parsley Field Mushrooms

Preparation time
20 minutes

Cooking time
20 minutes

Oven temperature
200C, 400F, Gas 6

Serves 6

Calories
170 per portion

You will need
450 g / 1 lb field mushrooms, stalks removed and sliced
75 g / 3 oz butter
2 garlic cloves, crushed
2 tablespoons chopped fresh parsley
6 tablespoons double cream
salt and pepper

Lightly grease six individual flameproof dishes or one 600 ml / 1 pint gratin dish. Arrange the mushrooms in the dishes or dish.

Melt the butter, add the garlic and stir well. Pour over the mushrooms. Mix together the parsley, cream and salt and pepper to taste, then pour over the mushrooms.

Cook in a preheated oven for 10 minutes for individual dishes or 15–20 minutes for the large dish. Serve hot. Hot wholemeal French bread to soak up the juices is an ideal accompaniment.

Cook's Tip

When some exotic varieties of mushrooms, such as oyster mushrooms, are available use them for a more pronounced flavour. Cut into thick strips for this dish.

Cook's Tip

Field mushrooms can contain insects so check them carefully before using. If in doubt, do not use.

155 | Burgundy Mushrooms

Preparation time
10 minutes, plus
marinating

Cooking time
20 minutes

Oven temperature
220C, 425F, Gas 7

Serves 4

Calories
323 per portion

You will need
3 tablespoons olive oil
1 onion, peeled and chopped
1 garlic clove, crushed
350 g / 12 oz button mushrooms,
 wiped
100 g / 4 oz cooked smoked ham,
 cut into strips
1 teaspoon mixed dried herbs
150 ml / ¼ pint Burgundy or other
 dry red wine
salt and pepper
chopped fresh parsley to garnish

Heat the oil and fry the onion and garlic for 3–5 minutes until soft.

Add the mushrooms, ham, herbs, red wine and salt and pepper to taste to the pan. Bring to the boil, then turn off the heat and leave to marinate for 30 minutes.

Divide the mushrooms and sauce between four individual ovenproof dishes and place in a preheated oven for 15 minutes until heated through. Garnish with parsley and serve. Hot French bread is an ideal accompaniment.

Cook's Tip

In the summer, prepare this dish in advance and serve as a cold starter or part of a salad lunch. For vegetarians, omit the ham.

156 | Mulled Mushrooms

Preparation time
10 minutes, plus chilling

Cooking time
15 minutes

Serves 4

Calories
490 per portion

You will need
2 tablespoons olive or corn oil
2 onions, peeled and thinly sliced
1 celery stick, thinly sliced
1 large garlic clove, peeled and
 crushed
2 rashers streaky bacon, rinded
 and chopped
150 ml / ¼ pint dry red wine
225 g / 8 oz tomatoes, skinned,
 quartered and seeded
1 tablespoon fresh thyme leaves,
 or 1½ teaspoons dried thyme
1 bay leaf
1 cinnamon stick (optional)
salt and pepper
450 g / 1 lb button mushrooms,
 wiped
1 tablespoon fresh thyme leaves
 to garnish (optional)

Heat the oil and fry the onions, celery, garlic and bacon for 5 minutes, stirring occasionally.

Stir in the wine, tomatoes, thyme, bay leaf, cinnamon stick and salt and pepper. Bring to the boil, then lower the heat.

Cut any large mushrooms into halves or quarters, but leave the rest whole. Add the mushrooms to the sauce in the pan. Simmer gently for 10 minutes. Leave to cool and remove the bay leaf and cinnamon stick.

Chill for at least one hour. Spoon onto individual plates. Serve sprinkled with the fresh thyme leaves if liked.

Cook's Tip

It isn't necessary to spend time peeling mushrooms. Instead, just wipe the caps with a damp cloth. Do not leave them to soak in bowl of water or they will become soggy.

157 | Shredded Courgettes

Preparation time
5 minutes

Cooking time
less than 1 minute

Serves 6

Calories
126 per portion

You will need
75 g / 3 oz butter
1 kg / 2 lb young courgettes, grated
salt and pepper

Melt the butter in a large frying pan or wok and stir-fry the courgettes over moderate heat for 35 seconds only until hot.

Add salt and pepper to taste and serve at once, before much juice runs, making them too wet.

158 | Courgette Fritters

Preparation time
30 minutes

Cooking time
20 minutes

Oven temperature
110C, 225F, Gas ¼

Serves 4

Calories
368 per portion

You will need
100 g / 4 oz wholemeal self-raising flour
½ teaspoon salt
pinch pepper
1 egg
1 tablespoon oil
2 teaspoons vinegar
150 ml / ¼ pint milk
5 small courgettes, about 275 g / 10 oz, cut into strips 5 mm × 5 cm / ¼ × 2 inches
oil for frying

For the dip
4 tablespoons mayonnaise
4 tablespoons plain yogurt
50 g / 2 oz blue cheese, crumbled
pepper

Whisk the flour, salt, pepper, egg, oil, vinegar and half the milk to a paste, then gradually add the remaining milk.

To make the dip, blend together the mayonnaise and yogurt, then fold in the cheese and season with plenty of pepper.

Heat the oven. Pour oil into a small pan. Heat the oil to 180–190C / 350–375F or until a cube of bread browns in 30 seconds.

Dip each piece of courgette into the batter, allowing any excess to run into the bowl, and then fry in small batches for 3 minutes until puffy and golden. Drain on paper towels and keep hot on a serving dish in the preheated oven until you have completed the frying. Sprinkle the fritters lightly with salt and serve hot with the dip.

Cook's Tip

If you don't have time for the last minute cooking, and would prefer to prepare this recipe in advance, salt the courgettes after grating them and leave to stand while the juice runs out. After 2 hours, squeeze them dry. Quickly cook in just butter and pepper, and put in a 150C, 300F, Gas 3 oven to keep warm. Because all the excess juice has been drawn out, the courgettes will remain crisp for up to 30 minutes.

Cook's Tip

Cauliflower florets can also be cooked following this recipe. Using wholemeal flour adds extra flavour but just white flour can be used as well.

159 | *Peperonata*

Preparation time
15 minutes

Cooking time
35 minutes

Serves 4

Calories
134 per portion

You will need
3 tablespoons oil
2 onions, peeled and finely
  chopped
2 garlic cloves, peeled and finely
  chopped
4 large red peppers, cored,
  seeded and cut into thin strips
500 g / 1¼lb tomatoes, skinned,
  seeded and neatly chopped
1 teaspoon chopped fresh basil, or
  ½ teaspoon dried
2 bay leaves
salt and pepper
2 tablespoons chopped fresh
  parsley

Heat the oil and fry the onions and garlic for 10 minutes until transparent. Add the peppers, stir well, then cover and cook over a low heat for 10 minutes until very tender.

Add the tomatoes, basil, bay leaves and salt and pepper to taste, then cover the pan again and continue cooking for 15 minutes over a low heat until all the vegetables are tender. Stir in the parsley and adjust the seasoning.

Serve hot or cold.

160 | *Leeks with Marjoram Sauce*

Preparation time
20 minutes

Cooking time
15 minutes

Serves 6

Calories
337 per portion

You will need
6 medium leeks

For the sauce
3 egg yolks
juice of 1 lemon
225 g / 8 oz butter, melted and
  cooled
1 tablespoon chopped fresh
  marjoram, or ½ tablespoon
  dried
salt and pepper

Thinly slice the leeks into rings, then wash in plenty of cold water.

Cook the leeks in boiling salted water, then drain well and keep warm while making the sauce.

To make the sauce, place the yolks and lemon juice in a heavy based pan. Whisk together over a very gentle heat until the mixture is thick and frothy. Do not let it boil or it will curdle. Remove from the heat, and very gradually whisk in the melted butter. (This can also be done in a liquidizer or food processor.) When all the butter is incorporated, add the marjoram and salt and pepper to taste.

Place the leeks in a warm serving dish and pour over the sauce. Serve at once.

Cook's Tip

To prevent crying while peeling onions, hold them under running cold water. Many varieties are available with skins which vary in colour from pale straw to golden brown. Buy onions which feel firm and dry with **light feathery skins. Store onions in a cool, dry place.**

Cook's Tip

Wash the leeks thoroughly to remove the sand and grit between the layers. Let soak in a bowl of water, then drain and rinse again.

161 | Fennel with Walnuts

Preparation time
10 minutes

Cooking time
1 minute

Serves 4

Calories
374 per portion

You will need
2 small fennel bulbs with leaves

For the dressing
4 tablespoons olive oil
1 garlic clove, peeled and crushed
 (optional)
100 g / 4 oz walnut halves,
 chopped
salt and pepper

Slice the fennel into thin, short strips, reserving the feathery leaves for garnish. Divide between four individual dishes.

To make the dressing, heat the olive oil and add the garlic and walnuts. Stir-fry for 1 minute until the walnuts are just beginning to brown. Add salt and pepper to taste, then spoon the hot dressing over the cold fennel.

Serve at once, garnished with the reserved fennel leaves.

162 | New Potatoes with Fennel and Mint

Preparation time
10 minutes

Cooking time
15–20 minutes

Serves 4

Calories
226 per portion

You will need
1 kg / 2 lb tiny new potatoes
1 tablespoon butter
1 small fennel bulb, finely chopped
pepper
2 tablespoons chopped fresh
 mint, plus extra sprigs to
 garnish

Place the potatoes in a pan of boiling salted water, then simmer for 15 minutes until tender. Drain well and keep warm.

Melt the butter in the warm pan. Add the fennel and fry for 5 minutes until just beginning to brown, then season well with pepper to taste.

Tip the potatoes into the pan, add the mint and toss the potatoes so they are coated with the butter, mint and fennel. Serve hot, garnished with sprigs of mint.

Cook's Tip

Aniseed-flavoured fennel, often called Florence fennel, is in season from August through November. Buy bulbs that are pale green or white. Avoid bulbs that are bruised or dark green.

Cook's Tip

New potatoes and mint are a classic combination. Fennel adds a complementary flavour and gives this traditional favourite a new twist. Jerusalem artichokes with new potatoes and mint would be equally tasty.

163 | *Russian-style Potatoes*

Preparation time
5 minutes

Cooking time
20 minutes

Serves 3

Calories
164 per portion

You will need
1 tablespoon butter
1 tablespoon oil
450 g / 1 lb small potatoes,
   unpeeled and thickly sliced
salt and pepper
2 spring onions, chopped

Heat the butter and oil until sizzling. Add the potatoes and fry quickly until golden brown but not cooked through.

Turn the slices and sprinkle generously with salt and pepper. Cover the pan, lower the heat and continue to fry/steam the slices for 20 minutes, shaking the pan occasionally to prevent them sticking, until tender.

Take the lid off the pan and turn up the heat again for a minute or two. Serve immediately, sprinkled with the spring onions.

Cook's Tip

Also known as kartoshki, this traditional Russian dish produces potatoes that taste as if they have been roasted without having to use the oven. This is a good side dish to serve with meat. Use the largest frying pan you have.

164 | *Celeriac Sticks with Mustard*

Preparation time
10 minutes

Cooking time
20–25 minutes

Serves 4

Calories
70 per portion

You will need
750 g / 1½ celeriac, peeled
salt
1 tablespoon lemon juice

For the sauce
150 ml / ¼ pint double or whipping
   cream, or plain yogurt
pepper
1 tablespoon whole grain mustard
lemon slices and parsley sprigs to
   garnish

Carefully cut the celeriac into chips about 1 x 7.5 cm / ½ x 3 inches.

Put the chips into a pan with a pinch of salt and the lemon juice and cover with water. Bring to the boil, cover and simmer for 15–20 minutes until the celeriac is tender but still firm. Drain and keep warm in a serving dish.

Pour the cream into the rinsed-out pan and stir in the salt and pepper to taste and mustard. Heat very gently until hot *but do not boil.*

Pour the sauce over the celeriac. Serve at once, garnished with lemon slices and parsley.

Cook's Tip

Celeriac looks like a knobbly swede with a turnip-like texture. As its name implies, it tastes like celery. If the cut flesh isn't coated with lemon juice, it will turn brown.

165 | Cauliflower with Peanut Sauce

Preparation time
25 minutes

Cooking time
15 minutes

Serves 4

Calories
227 per portion

You will need
1 cauliflower, about 500 g / 1¼ lb, cut into florets
salt
2 tablespoons chopped salted peanuts to garnish

For the sauce
1 tablespoon butter
1 tablespoon plain flour
150 ml / ¼ pint milk
150 ml / ¼ pint vegetable stock
4 tablespoons crunchy peanut butter
½ teaspoon yeast extract
pepper

Cook the cauliflower in boiling salted water for 6–8 minutes, until tender but still crisp. Drain and keep warm in a serving dish.

Meanwhile, to make the sauce, melt the butter, add the flour and cook for 3 minutes, stirring constantly. Pour in the milk and vegetable stock and bring to the boil, stirring. Simmer for 2–3 minutes, then stir in the peanut butter, a spoonful at a time. The peanut butter will thicken the sauce. Add the yeast extract, a little salt if necessary (there is probably enough in the peanut butter) and pepper to taste.

Pour the sauce over the cauliflower and sprinkle with the chopped peanuts. Serve hot.

166 | Lemon Cabbage with Poppy Seeds

Preparation time
5 minutes

Cooking time
10–15 minutes

Serves 4

Calories
123 per portion

You will need
150 ml / ¼ pint water
½ teaspoon salt
350 g / 12 oz white cabbage, shredded
350 g / 12 oz spring greens or green cabbage, shredded
25 g / 1 oz butter, diced
grated rind of 1 lemon
1½ teaspoons poppy seeds
pepper
2–3 tablespoons soured cream to serve (optional)

Boil the water and salt. Add both white and green cabbages, cover and simmer steadily for 7–10 minutes until tender but still crisp and most of the water absorbed.

Uncover and boil quickly to reduce any remaining liquid. Add the butter, lemon rind, poppy seeds and lots of black pepper. Stir briefly until the butter is melted and the cabbage well coated.

Spoon the hot cabbage into a warm dish and serve with soured cream spooned over the top if liked.

Cook's Tip

Available all year round, cauliflowers should be eaten within a day of purchase. Buy firm heads, as any rubberiness indicates they are not fresh. Wrap in cling film or foil and store in the salad drawer of the refrigerator. For this recipe the florets can also be steamed rather than boiled.

Cook's Tip

Use a pastry brush to get all the grated lemon rind off the back of the grater.

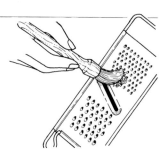

167 | Beetroot with Soured Cream and Cumin

Preparation time
5 minutes

Cooking time
5 minutes

Serves 4

Calories
119 per portion

You will need
25 g / 1 oz butter
2 teaspoons ground cumin
150 ml / ¼ pint soured cream
450 g / 1 lb beetroot, peeled and
   diced
salt and pepper

Melt the butter, sprinkle in the cumin and cook for 1–2 minutes, stirring.

Add the soured cream, beetroot and salt and pepper to taste. Cook until the beetroot is heated through, stirring gently. Transfer to a warmed serving dish and serve at once.

168 | Mixed Winter Vegetables

Preparation time
10 minutes

Cooking time
1 hour

Oven temperature
190C, 375F, Gas 5

Serves 4

Calories
50 per portion

You will need
500 g / 1¼ lb peeled mixed winter
   root vegetables, diced
salt and pepper
1 tablespoon butter or margarine
2–3 tomatoes, sliced
watercress sprigs to garnish

Put the vegetables into a casserole with water to cover, salt and pepper to taste and the butter. Cover and cook for 1 hour until very tender.

Strain the vegetables and place in individual serving dishes. Add the tomato slices, garnish with watercress and serve at once.

Cook's Tip

The ground cumin can be replaced with dried dill weed or 1 tablespoon chopped fresh dill. Grated orange rind also adds extra flavour.

Cook's Tip

Try to dice the vegetables to the same size so they cook in the same time. Use potatoes, carrots, swedes, parsnips and turnips. For added fibre, do not peel the potatoes and carrots.

Salads

It doesn't take long to create a salad that is so much more than just a bowl of lettuce leaves. The contrast of different colours and flavours that gives appetite appeal is easy with a little inspiration. This chapter includes recipes that make the most of meat and seafood as well as vegetables, and a selection of dressing recipes. There are ideas for side salads, starter and main course salads, some filling enough to make a light meal.

169 | Green and Gold Salad

Preparation time
25 minutes

Serves 4

Calories
476 per portion

You will need
1 ripe avocado
1 tablespoon lemon juice
8 slices French loaf
oil for shallow frying
1 small Cos or Webb lettuce, torn into pieces
4 hard-boiled eggs, shelled and quartered
1 bunch watercress
25 g / 1 oz Parmesan cheese, grated to serve

For the dressing
6 tablespoons olive oil
1 tablespoon lemon juice
1 garlic clove, peeled and crushed (optional)
salt and pepper
2–3 drops Tabasco sauce

Halve, stone and peel the avocado, then cut the flesh into slices and brush with lemon juice.

Cut each slice of bread into quarters. Heat the oil and fry quickly for 1 minute until golden. Drain the croûtons on paper towels and set aside.

Place the avocado, lettuce and hard-boiled eggs in a large bowl, then add the croûtons and watercress.

To make the dressing, whisk together the oil, lemon juice, garlic, salt and pepper to taste, and Tabasco until blended. Pour over the salad and toss lightly to coat thoroughly. Sprinkle with Parmesan cheese and serve.

Cook's Tip

Add a nutty flavour to this salad by replacing the olive oil with walnut oil and adding chopped walnut halves to the salad.

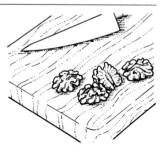

170 | French Salad

Preparation time
15 minutes

Serves 4

Calories
334 per portion

You will need
selection of salad leaves, such as Webb and curly endive, well rinsed
1 red pepper, cored, seeded and cut into thin strips
12 black olives, stoned
½ cucumber, thinly sliced
2 tablespoons chopped fresh chives

For the dressing
1 teaspoon Dijon mustard
150 ml / ¼ pint olive oil
4 tablespoons wine vinegar
pinch sugar
salt and pepper

To make the dressing, put all the ingredients in a jar and shake until well blended.

To serve, mix together all the salad ingredients and pour over the dressing. Toss until all the vegetables are well coated, then arrange on a large serving plate. Serve at once.

Cook's Tip

The lettuce leaves will remain crisp after rinsing and shaken dry if kept in a polythene bag in the refrigerator. Once the dressing is added, serve at once.

171 | Spring Mixed Salad with Honey Dressing

Preparation time
30 minutes

Serves 6

Calories
153 per portion

You will need
1 curly endive lettuce, washed, dried and broken into pieces
6 small tomatoes, cut into wedges
1 bunch spring onions, chopped
1 bunch radishes, sliced
2 hard-boiled eggs, shelled and chopped
1 × 326-g / 11½-oz can sweetcorn kernels, well drained

For the dressing
2 tablespoons runny honey
1 tablespoon lemon juice
1 teaspoon French mustard
2 tablespoons olive oil
salt and pepper

Line a large salad bowl with the curly endive. Arrange the tomato wedges around the edge of the bowl. Sprinkle with the spring onions, radishes and the eggs.

Reserve 2 tablespoons of the sweetcorn kernels for the dressing, then add the remainder to the salad.

To make the dressing, blend all the ingredients together in a liquidizer or food processor, including the reserved sweetcorn kernels.

Pour the dressing over the salad when ready to serve.

172 | Spinach and Ham Salad with Blue Cheese Dressing

Preparation time
15 minutes

Serves 4

Calories
301 per portion

You will need
275 g / 10 oz fresh spinach leaves, washed and stalks removed
225 g / 8 oz smoked ham, cut into thin strips
1 large avocado
1 tablespoon lemon juice

For the dressing
100 g / 4 oz blue cheese, crumbled
150 ml / ¼ pint mayonnaise
salt and pepper

Finely shred the spinach leaves and place in a large salad or serving bowl. Add half of the ham and toss to mix.

Halve, stone and peel the avocado, then slice. Mix with the lemon juice and arrange attractively over the spinach and ham mixture.

To make the dressing, place the cheese in a bowl and beat until smooth and creamy. Gradually blend in the mayonnaise to make a smooth and thickened dressing. Season with salt and pepper to taste. Spoon over the avocado, then sprinkle with the remaining ham. Serve at once.

Cook's Tip

Curly endive is a frizzy salad green with a slightly bitter taste now widely available at greengrocers and supermarkets. If you can't find it, substitute crisp Cos lettuce or Chinese leaves.

Cook's Tip

Take great care when adding salt to the salad dressing. Blue cheese can be very salty and the dressing may not need any additional salt. Stilton, Danish blue, Dolcelatte or Roquefort are each suitable cheeses for this salad.

173 | *Leek, Orange and Hazelnut Salad*

Preparation time
10 minutes, plus marinating

Serves 4

Calories
276 per portion

You will need
450 g / 1 lb leeks
50 g / 2 oz shelled hazelnuts, toasted and chopped

For the dressing
2 medium oranges
4 tablespoons olive oil
salt and pepper

Slice the leeks into rounds as thinly as possible. Wash well, then separate into rings and drain.

To make the dressing, cut the orange rinds into long thin strips and place in a large bowl. Add the juice from the oranges, the olive oil and salt and pepper to taste.

Whisk the dressing together and then add the leeks to the bowl. Toss until all the leeks are coated in dressing.

Marinate for at least 1 hour to soften the leeks. Stir in the hazelnuts just before serving. This salad goes particularly well with chicken and lamb.

174 | *Chicory and Orange Salad*

Preparation time
15 minutes

Serves 4

Calories
118 per portion

You will need
3 large or 4 small heads chicory
3 medium oranges
1 shallot or small onion, peeled and cut in rings
4 tablespoons French dressing
6 large or 8 small stuffed olives to garnish

Cut the chicory crosswise into slices and place in a salad bowl.

Cut away the peel and pith from the oranges. Cut the flesh into segments and add to the chicory, squeezing in any juice as well.

Pour the French dressing over and toss well. Scatter the stuffed olives on top. This is a good accompaniment to salamis and cold meats.

Cook's Tip

This is a good winter salad.
If the leeks are very strong tasting, blanching them for 1 minute will give them a milder flavour. Drain well before adding to the dressing.

Cook's Tip

The sharp, bitter taste of chicory is off-set by the fresh-tasting, juicy oranges in this salad. Store chicory leaves in a polythene bag in the salad drawer of your refrigerator; they should keep for about a week.

175 | Fennel and Apple Salad

Preparation time
15 minutes

Serves 4

Calories
241 per portion

You will need
2 small bulbs fennel, about 450 g / 1 lb
4 small or 3 large dessert apples
50 g / 2 oz shelled hazelnuts, roughly chopped
150 ml / ¼ pint mayonnaise
5 tablespoons orange juice
salt and pepper

Cut the fennel bulbs in half lengthways. Trim off the feathery green leaves from the tops and reserve for the garnish. Slice the fennel very finely and put in a large bowl.

Quarter the apples, remove the cores and cut into thin slices. Add the apples and hazelnuts to the fennel.

Spoon the mayonnaise into a large bowl or jug, add the orange juice and blend until smooth. Add salt and pepper to taste. Pour over the salad and toss until all the ingredients are thoroughly coated.

Garnish with the reserved fennel leaves. This is good with cold roast meat or with whole, cold poached fish.

176 | Crunchy Mixed Salad

Preparation time
10 minutes

Serves 4

Calories
64 per portion

You will need
2 oranges
2 carrots
2 tablespoons raisins
1 dessert apple, cored and roughly grated
¼ cauliflower, broken into florets
2 celery sticks, chopped

For the dressing
3 tablespoons oil
1 tablespoon cider vinegar
¼ teaspoon soft light brown sugar
1½ teaspoons English mustard
salt and pepper

To make the dressing, place all the ingredients in a screw-top jar and shake well to combine.

Peel and segment the oranges, carefully removing all the bitter white pith. Finely grate the carrots.

Place the oranges, carrots, raisins, apple, cauliflower and celery in a salad bowl. Add the dressing and toss well to coat. Serve at once or cover and chill.

Cook's Tip

This is a salad that is best assembled just before serving so the ingredients retain their crisp and crunchy textures. For extra zest, add the grated rind of one orange to the mayonnaise.

Cook's Tip

The leftover cauliflower can quickly be made into a filling soup. Cook it in 900 ml / 1½ pints chicken or vegetable stock with a bay leaf and onion slices until very tender. Remove the bay leaf. Purée, then gently reheat with 150 ml / ¼ pint double cream and season with salt and pepper to taste. To serve, ladle the soup into individual bowls and top each portion with very finely chopped fresh parsley or snipped chives and finely grated Cheddar cheese.

177 | Orchard Salad

Preparation time
15 minutes

Serves 4

Calories
175 per portion

You will need
grated rind and juice of 2 small
oranges
1 tablespoon chopped fresh mint
or parsley
salt and pepper
350 g / 12 oz firm pears
350 g / 12 oz dessert apples, such
as Cox's or Worcesters
100 g / 4 oz blackberries
50 g / 2 oz shelled hazelnuts with
skins, roughly chopped

Place the orange rind and juice in a bowl. Stir in the herbs
and salt and pepper to taste.

Quarter and core the pears and apples. Cut each
quarter crosswise into wedge-shaped slices. Add to the
orange juice and toss well.

Add the blackberries and hazelnuts to the other fruit
and toss all together. This salad goes well with rich
meats such as pork and duck.

178 | Orange Winter Salad

Preparation time
15 minutes

Serves 4

Calories
327 per portion

You will need
4 large oranges
1 × 400-g / 14-oz can red kidney
beans, drained and rinsed
275 g / 10 oz bean-sprouts
4 sticks celery, thinly sliced
watercress sprigs to garnish

For the dressing
5 tablespoons olive oil
2 tablespoons lemon juice
¼ teaspoon sugar
¼ teaspoon English mustard
salt and pepper

Peel the oranges, removing all the pith, then segment,
cutting down either side of each membrane. Put in a
bowl with any juice that runs out while cutting.

Add the beans, bean-sprouts and celery and toss
gently together.

To make the dressing, put the oil, lemon juice, sugar,
mustard and salt and pepper to taste, into a screw-top jar
and shake until blended.

Just before serving the salad, spoon the dressing over
and garnish with watercress.

Cook's Tip

**Adding the cut apples and
pears to the orange juice
prevents the fruits' flesh from
turning brown.**

**Assemble this salad at the
last minute so the fruits retain
their textures and the
hazelnuts do not become soft.**

Cook's Tip

**Dried kidney beans can be
used instead of the canned
variety. Soak the beans
overnight in water to cover,
then drain and cover again
with fresh water. Boil for 10
minutes, then simmer for
35–40 minutes until tender.**

179 | Peaches and Cream Salad

Preparation time
10 minutes

Serves 4

Calories
494 per portion

You will need
225 g / 8 oz full fat soft cheese
1–2 tablespoons single cream or
  milk (optional)
salt and pepper
100 g / 4 oz mixed nuts, chopped
  and toasted
lettuce leaves
4 ripe peaches or nectarines,
  halved and stoned, weighing
  together 500–600 g / 1¼–1½ lb
1 × 50-g / 2-oz jar caviar or
  lumpfish roe to garnish
  (optional)

Beat the cheese until smooth and if necessary thin it down with a little cream or milk. Add salt and pepper to taste. Stir in half the nuts.

Divide the lettuce leaves between individual plates, and place the peach halves on top.

Spoon some cream cheese filling into the centre of each peach half and sprinkle the reserved nuts over the top. Garnish each serving with a spoonful of caviar or lumpfish roe, if liked.

180 | Pears in Stilton

Preparation time
10 minutes

Serves 4

Calories
174 per portion

You will need
150 ml / 5 fl oz plain yogurt
100 g / 4 oz blue Stilton cheese
salt and pepper
1 small lettuce
4 ripe pears
1 bunch watercress to garnish

Blend the yogurt with half the blue Stilton cheese until smooth. Add salt and pepper to taste.

Arrange a bed of lettuce leaves on individual plates. Core and slice the pears, decoratively arranging one pear on each plate.

Spoon the dressing over the pear slices and top with the remaining cheese, either crumbled or grated. Garnish each plate with a few sprigs of watercress. Serve at once.

Cook's Tip

When buying fresh peaches, avoid any which are bruised or feel too soft and give when lightly squeezed. You can prepare the filling in advance and keep it covered in the refrigerator, but only assemble the salad just before serving or the peach flesh may become discoloured.

Cook's Tip

Blue Stilton is a traditional English cheese. Danish blue is more economical and may be used but the flavour will be different. For a more substantial salad, add one crumbled, crisply grilled bacon rasher to each portion.

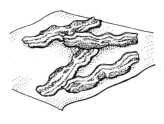

181 | Pear Waldorf Salad

Preparation time
25 minutes

Serves 4

Calories
171 per portion

You will need
1 lettuce, shredded
2 sticks celery, chopped
1 red pepper, cored and sliced
25 g / 1 oz walnut halves
75 g / 3 oz green grapes, peeled, halved and seeded
1 dessert pear, peeled, cored and sliced
225 g / 8 oz smoked chicken, skinned and boned

For the dressing
2 tablespoons plain yogurt
2 tablespoons mayonnaise
2 tablespoons grated cucumber
1 teaspoon grated onion
½ teaspoon chopped fresh tarragon

For the garnish
1 dessert pear, cored and sliced
few sprigs fresh tarragon

Mix the lettuce with the celery, red pepper, walnuts, grapes, pear and smoked chicken.

To make the dressing, mix the yogurt with the mayonnaise, add the remaining ingredients and blend well.

Just before serving, spoon the dressing over the salad and toss well to mix. Garnish with slices of pear and a few sprigs of fresh tarragon.

Cook's Tip

This is a variation on a classic Waldorf salad, which is made with apples. The dressing can be made up to three days in advance, then tossed with the salad ingredients just before serving.

182 | Tuscan Nectarine and Avocado Salad

Preparation time
10 minutes

Serves 4
as a starter

Calories
253 per portion

You will need
2 fresh nectarines, blanched and peeled
1 avocado, halved and stoned
225 g / 8 oz mixed salad leaves
8–12 small cherry tomatoes

For the dressing
5 tablespoons olive oil
5 teaspoons tarragon vinegar
1 garlic clove, peeled and crushed
1 teaspoon whole grain mustard
1 teaspoon chopped fresh tarragon
1 teaspoon chopped fresh chives
salt and pepper

Slice the nectarines thinly and place in a large salad bowl. Cut the avocado into small balls using a melon baller or teaspoon and add to the nectarines. Add the mixed salad leaves and tomatoes, tossing gently to blend, taking care not to break up the avocado balls.

To make the dressing, beat the oil and vinegar together until well blended and lightly thickened. Add the garlic, mustard, tarragon, chives and salt and pepper to taste, blending well. Spoon over the salad and toss lightly to mix. Serve at once with chunks of wholemeal or granary bread.

Cook's Tip

Curly endive, lamb's lettuce, radicchio and chicory leaves are all suitable for using in this salad. Supermarkets now stock a greater variety of salad greens.

183 | *Avocado Salad*

Preparation time
20 minutes

Serves 4
as a light main salad

Calories
333 per portion

You will need
4 large lettuce leaves
4 tablespoons olive oil
2 tablespoons white wine vinegar
salt and pepper
2 avocados
4 tomatoes, skinned and chopped
225 g / 8 oz Mozzarella cheese,
*   sliced*
1 teaspoon dried oregano

Arrange the lettuce leaves on four plates and set aside.

Whisk together the oil, vinegar and salt and pepper to taste. Halve, stone and peel the avocados.

Place an avocado half in the centre of each plate, then arrange the tomato and Mozzarella slices on either side. Spoon the dressing over the top of each and sprinkle with the oregano. Serve at once.

184 | *Greek Salad with Tahini Dressing*

Preparation time
15 minutes

Serves 4

Calories
180 per portion

You will need
½ cucumber
350 g / 12 oz tomatoes, cut into
*   thin wedges*
1 small green pepper, quartered,
*   seeded and sliced*
1 small onion, peeled and thinly
*   sliced*
8 small black olives, stoned and
*   halved*
100 g / 4 oz feta cheese, cubed

For the dressing
2 tablespoons tahini paste
4 tablespoons plain yogurt
1–2 tablespoons water
2 tablespoons chopped fresh
*   parsley*
1 small garlic clove, crushed
*   (optional)*
salt and pepper

Cut the cucumber into 5 mm / ¼ inch slices, then cut across into 5 mm / ¼ inch batons. Place in a salad bowl. Add the tomatoes, green peppers, onions and olives.

To make the dressing, place the tahini paste in a small bowl. Slowly beat in the yogurt and thin with the water as needed. Stir in the parsley, garlic, and salt and pepper to taste. Pour over the salad and toss well. Sprinkle the feta cheese over. This salad goes well with cold roast meats and pitta bread.

Cook's Tip

This multi-colour salad is also an excellent starter if you use half the amount of ingredients. Slice the avocado halves and arrange with the tomato and cheese slices. Fresh chives and marjoram also add interesting flavours.

Cook's Tip

Tahini paste is made from finely ground sesame seeds and is available in jars from supermarkets and delicatessens. It gives a distinctive flavour to this dressing.

Feta cheese, made from sheep's milk, is a salty white cheese popular in Greece and throughout the Middle East. Because the feta is so salty, take care when adding salt to the dressing.

185 | Courgette, Pepper and Tomato Salad

Preparation time
15 minutes

Cooking time
2–3 minutes

Serves 6

Calories
83 per portion

You will need
450 g / 1 lb small courgettes
225 g / 8 oz tomatoes, skinned and quartered
1 red pepper, cored, seeded and diced
1 green pepper, cored, seeded and diced

For the dressing
3 tablespoons oil
juice of 1 lemon
2 teaspoons dried oregano
salt and pepper

Slice the courgettes. Put them into a pan of lightly salted water and boil for 2–3 minutes. Strain and rinse under cold water to stop the cooking.

Place the courgettes in a large bowl with the tomatoes and pepper.

To make the dressing, mix together the oil, lemon juice, oregano and salt and pepper to taste. Pour over the vegetables and toss lightly. Serve at once.

186 | Cucumber Salad with Honey

Preparation time
10 minutes, plus draining

Serves 4

Calories
76 per portion

You will need
1 cucumber, peeled and cut into chunks
salt
4 spring onions, finely chopped
spring onion tassels to garnish

For the dressing
4 teaspoons clear honey
4 teaspoons lemon juice
4 tablespoons olive oil
1 teaspoon chopped fresh marjoram (optional)
pepper

Place the cucumber in a colander over a bowl and sprinkle with 2 tablespoons of salt. Leave to stand for 30 minutes to drain off excess liquid. Pat dry with paper towels.

Combine the cucumber and spring onions in a serving bowl.

To make the dressing, place all the ingredients in a screw-top jar and shake until well blended.

Pour the dressing over the salad just before serving. Toss well. Serve garnished with spring onion tassels.

Cook's Tip

Olive oil is a good flavoured oil to use in this Mediterranean-style salad. Fresh marjoram or chervil are good substitutes for the oregano; if using a fresh herb, double the quantity.

Cook's Tip

For extra colour, do not peel the cucumber. Serve as a side salad with cold roast chicken or cold cooked ham.

187 | Sweet-and-Sour Cucumber

Preparation time
10 minutes, plus salting

Serves 4

Calories
177 per portion

You will need
1 cucumber, sliced
salt
coriander sprig and shredded lime
    rind to garnish

For the dressing
1 small onion, peeled and finely
    chopped
2 tablespoons white wine vinegar
1 tablespoon clear honey
5 tablespoons oil
2 tablespoons tomato purée
1 tablespoon English mustard
salt and pepper

Place the cucumber in a colander and sprinkle with salt. Put a plate on top and leave for 30 minutes.

Rinse the cucumber and dry well with paper towels. Arrange on individual plates.

To make the dressing, mix together all the ingredients until well blended. Spoon over the cucumber. Garnish each plate with coriander and chill until ready to serve.

188 | Cucumber, Melon and Ham Salad

Preparation time
25 minutes

Serves 4
as a starter

Calories
160 per portion

You will need
1 Ogen or small honeydew melon
1 slice cooked ham, about 225 g /
    8 oz, cut into thin matchstick
    strips
4 tomatoes, quartered
75 g / 3 oz black grapes, halved
    and seeded
½ cucumber, very thinly sliced
mint sprigs to garnish

For the dressing
4 tablespoons soured cream
2 tablespoons chopped spring
    onions
1 teaspoon chopped fresh mint
salt and pepper

Halve the melon, then scoop out the seeds and discard. Remove the flesh with a melon baller or cut into bite-sized cubes. Reserve the melon shells for serving if wished.

Place the ham in a bowl with the melon, tomatoes, grapes and cucumber, tossing gently to mix.

To make the dressing, mix the soured cream with the spring onion, mint and salt and pepper to taste.

Mix the salad ingredients with the dressing, tossing gently to mix. Return to the melon shells to serve. Garnish with a few sprigs of mint before serving.

Cook's Tip

Leaving the cucumber to stand with salt draws out moisture so the final dish isn't too watery. It is a French technique known as 'degorger', and it also removes any bitter flavours.

Cook's Tip

Seedless green grapes are a good alternative for the black grapes in this recipe.

189 | Broad Bean and Bacon Salad

Preparation time	**You will need**
10 minutes	450 g / 1 lb shelled broad beans
	salt
Cooking time	4 rashers streaky bacon, rinded, to
5–10 minutes	garnish
Serves 6	For the dressing
	2 tablespoons chopped fresh
Calories	parsley
136 per portion	150 ml / 5 fl oz plain yogurt
	pepper

Put the broad beans into a pan with a little salt. Pour over just enough boiling water to cover and simmer for 5 minutes until tender. Drain and rinse under cold water to cool quickly.

Grill the bacon until crispy. Drain and cool.

To make the dressing, stir the parsley into the yogurt and add salt and pepper to taste.

Stir the dressing into the beans. Turn the bean salad into a serving dish and crumble the crispy bacon over the top. This is an especially good accompaniment to cold roast lamb.

190 | Gado Gado

Preparation time	**You will need**
15 minutes	100 g / 4 oz cabbage, shredded
	100 g / 4 oz French beans, cut into
Cooking time	4 cm / 1½ inch lengths
15–20 minutes	100 g / 4 oz carrots, sliced
	100 g / 4 oz cauliflower, divided
Serves 6	into small florets
	salt
Calories	50 g / 2 oz bean-sprouts
147 per portion	2 hard-boiled eggs, shelled and
	sliced (optional)
	50 g / 2 oz salted peanuts to
	garnish

For the sauce
4 tablespoons crunchy peanut butter
juice of 1 lemon
4 tablespoons water
few drops Tabasco sauce
pepper

Simmer the cabbage, beans, carrots and cauliflower separately in boiling salted water for a few minutes until just tender. Rinse under cold water to cool quickly.

To make the sauce, place the peanut butter in a bowl. Blend in the lemon juice and then the water until well mixed. Stir in enough Tabasco sauce to make a spicy sauce, and then add salt and pepper.

Combine the vegetables and the bean-sprouts and arrange in a shallow serving dish. Lay the slices of hard-boiled egg over the top, if liked, and pour the peanut sauce over the centre of the salad. Sprinkle with the salted peanuts.

Cook's Tip

Broad beans are in season from late May to early September. Very young ones have tender skins that can be eaten with the beans but older beans have tough outer skins; these may be difficult to remove. If necessary, drop the podded bean in boiling water for a few minutes, then drain and rub off the skin with a tea towel. Broad beans are also available tinned and frozen.

Cook's Tip

This crunchy vegetable salad is Indonesian. For a more authentic flavour, add grated fresh coconut or desiccated coconut to the sauce.

191 | Crunchy Green Salad

Preparation time
25 minutes

Serves 4

Calories
212 per portion

You will need
100 g / 4 oz green cabbage
100 g / 4 oz broccoli
100 g / 4 oz courgettes
1 small green pepper
1 stick celery, thinly sliced

For the dressing
150 ml / ¼ pint plain yogurt or
   soured cream
1 tablespoon white wine vinegar
salt and black pepper
2 tablespoons crumbled blue
   cheese, such as Danish blue,
   Stilton or Roquefort

Slice the green cabbage very thinly, discarding any core. Wash, drain and place in a bowl.

Divide the broccoli into florets, cutting away the coarse central stalks and slicing down the thin stalks and heads. Wash, drain and add to the bowl.

Top and tail the courgettes and slice as thinly as possible. Add to the bowl.

Cut the pepper into halves or quarters, remove the core and seeds, and slice very thinly. Add to the bowl with the celery.

To make the dressing, blend the yogurt or soured cream, vinegar and salt and pepper in a liquidizer or food processor. Stir in the cheese. Pour over the vegetables and toss well. Marinate for 1 hour before serving.

192 | Red Cabbage Salad

Preparation time
15 minutes

Serves 4

Calories
263 per portion

You will need
350 g / 12 oz red cabbage
1 large Cox's apple
2 sticks celery, chopped
50 g / 2 oz seedless raisins
50 g / 2 oz walnut halves chopped

For the dressing
3 tablespoons mayonnaise
1 tablespoon white wine vinegar
1 tablespoon oil
1 garlic clove, peeled and crushed
1 teaspoon clear honey
1 teaspoon whole grain mustard
salt and pepper

Cut away the cabbage's core, then finely shred, using a sharp knife or food processor. Quarter and core the apple, then cut into small pieces.

Mix together the cabbage, apple, celery, raisins and walnuts.

To make the dressing, mix all the ingredients together. Pour over the salad and mix thoroughly. Serve at once or cover and chill.

Cook's Tip

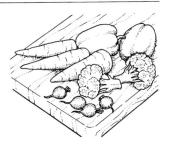

Another colourful combination of vegetables that goes well with this piquant cheese dressing is thinly sliced carrots, diced red and yellow peppers, thinly sliced radishes and small cauliflower florets.

Cook's Tip

This salad remains crisp even if made a day ahead. Make sure the apples are well coated with the dressing so they don't discolour.

193 | *Beetroot and Orange Salad*

Preparation time
10 minutes

Serves 4

Calories
122 per portion

You will need
450 g / 1 lb cooked beetroot, skinned
150 ml / 5 fl oz soured cream
1 medium orange, halved crosswise
2 tablespoons snipped fresh chives
salt and pepper

Cut the beetroot into 1 cm / ½ inch dice and arrange in a shallow serving dish.

Put the soured cream into a bowl. Add the grated rind and juice from half the orange. Cut the peel and pith away from the remaining orange half and cut the flesh into segments. Cut each segment in half.

Scatter the orange segments over the beetroot.

Mix the chives, salt and pepper with the soured cream. Spoon this dressing over the beetroot and oranges, but do not stir. Serve at once.

194 | *Beetroot and Radish Salad*

Preparation time
20 minutes

Serves 4

Calories
94 per portion

You will need
225 g / 8 oz raw young beetroot, peeled and finely grated
few onion rings (red onions if possible)
½ bunch radishes, thinly sliced

For the dressing
2 tablespoons olive oil
1 tablespoon red wine vinegar
½ teaspoon mustard
pinch sugar
salt and pepper
1 teaspoon chopped fresh mint (optional)

Place the beetroot in a serving bowl and sprinkle with onion rings. Add the radishes.

To make the dressing, place all the ingredients in a screw-top jar and shake until well mixed.

Pour the dressing over the salad just before serving. Serve, garnished with fresh mint.

Cook's Tip

The dressing is spooned over this salad, rather than being mixed with the beetroot and oranges, to preserve the vibrant colours. Beetroot 'bleeds' and if all the ingredients are combined, the salad will be pink.

Cook's Tip

Choose small, firm beetroot for this recipe because they have the sweetest flavour. Fresh beetroot is available all year round.

195 | Potato and Mortadella Salad

Preparation time
20 minutes

Cooking time
15 minutes

Serves 4

Calories
443 per portion

You will need
450 g / 1 lb small potatoes, washed
salt and pepper
6–8 spring onions, thinly sliced
2 tablespoons chopped fresh chives
1 tablespoon chopped fresh chervil or parsley
125 ml / 4 fl oz soured cream
1 tablespoon white wine vinegar
175 g / 6 oz mortadella, in one piece, skinned

Cook the potatoes in boiling salted water until just tender. Drain and, when cool enough to handle, rub off the skins. Slice the potatoes thickly or cut in quarters.

Stir the onions and herbs into the soured cream, then stir in the vinegar and season well with pepper. Toss the potatoes in this mixture.

Cut four thin slices of sausage to garnish. Cube the remainder.

Cut from the edge to the centre of each slice of mortadella and wrap it into a cone. Just before serving, stir the cubed mortadella carefully into the potato salad. Spoon it into a dish and garnish with the four cones.

196 | Hot Potato Salad

Preparation time
10 minutes

Cooking time
10–15 minutes

Serves 4

Calories
311 per portion

You will need
450 g / 1 lb waxy potatoes
1 onion, peeled and chopped
1 tablespoon boiling water
1 tablespoon white wine vinegar
3 tablespoons mayonnaise
2 tablespoons single cream
salt and pepper
1 tablespoon chopped fresh parsley

Peel and cut the potatoes into 1 cm / ½ inch cubes. Boil in salted water until just cooked and still holding their shapes.

Meanwhile, place the onion in a large bowl, with the boiling water and vinegar. Strain the potatoes and add to the onion with the mayonnaise, cream and add salt and pepper to taste. Reheat gently if necessary.

Transfer to a warm serving bowl. Sprinkle with parsley and serve at once.

Cook's Tip

Mortadella is a variety of pork sausage that has been made in Italy for centuries. It has a smooth texture and is best served thinly sliced.

Cook's Tip

Serve this German-style potato salad as an accompaniment to roast chicken or meatloaf.

197 | *Tabbouleh*

Preparation time
10 minutes, plus
soaking

Serves 8

Calories
324 per portion

You will need
350 g / 12 oz bulghar (cracked
    wheat)
2 bunches spring onions, finely
    chopped
1 large bunch fresh parsley,
    chopped
1 large bunch fresh mint, chopped
juice of 2 lemons
150 ml / ¼ pint olive oil
salt and pepper

Place the bulghar in a large bowl and cover with plenty of
cold water. Soak for 1 hour. Strain well, pressing out as
much water as possible.

   Put the bulghar back into the bowl and add the spring
onions, parsley, mint, lemon juice, olive oil, salt and pepper. Mix well. Cover and chill until ready to serve.

198 | *Lentil and Tomato Salad*

Preparation time
15 minutes

Cooking time
30 minutes

Serves 4

Calories
322 per portion

You will need
225 g/ 8 oz green lentils
1 small onion, peeled and finely
    chopped
900 ml / 1½ pints water
1 bay leaf
salt
6 tablespoons vinaigrette
225 g / 8 oz tomatoes, chopped
1 small green pepper, cored,
    seeded and diced
4 spring onions, chopped
8 black olives, stoned and
    chopped
1 tablespoon chopped fresh
    parsley

Place the lentils and chopped onion in a saucepan with
the water, bay leaf and some salt. Bring to the boil. Cover
and simmer for 30 minutes until the lentils are tender but
not mushy.

   Drain the lentils and place in a salad bowl. Stir in the
vinaigrette while they are still warm and leave to cool.

   Stir in the tomatoes, green pepper, spring onions and
black olives. Sprinkle with the parsley and serve.

Cook's Tip

**Bulghar, or cracked wheat, is
grain which has been steamed
and toasted. Consequently it
has a slightly nutty taste. It is
the traditional ingredient of
this Lebanese salad.**

Cook's Tip

**French dressing or vinaigrette
is a classic combination of oil,
vinegar and flavourings. It is
widely available , but you can
make your own. Combine 2
tablespoons white wine
vinegar or lemon juice and 6
tablespoons oil in a screw-top**
**jar with a pinch of mustard
powder and salt and pepper
to taste. Shake well.
Alternatively, whisk all the
ingredients together in a small
bowl. The dressing will keep
for at least one week in the
refrigerator.**

199 | *Inca Salad*

Preparation time
10 minutes, plus chilling

Serves 4

Calories
318 per portion

You will need
*4 tablespoons French dressing
few drops Tabasco sauce
2 medium avocados
350 g / 12 oz potato, peeled,
   cooked and cubed
1 × 200-g / 7-oz can tuna fish,
   drained and flaked
1 lettuce (optional)
4 small fresh chilli peppers cut
   into 'flowers' or cucumber
   slices to garnish*

To make a hot chilli dressing, pour the French dressing into a bowl and blend in Tabasco sauce to taste.

Cut the avocados in half, then remove the stones and peel. Cut the flesh into small cubes and lightly toss in the dressing.

Add the potato to the avocado with the tuna fish. Toss gently, making sure that the avocado does not get mashed.

Line a serving dish with lettuce leaves if liked, and pile the avocado salad on top. Garnish with chilli 'flowers' or cucumber slices.

200 | *Pickled Herring Salad*

Preparation time
20 minutes

Serves 4

Calories
234 per portion

You will need
*1 × 340-ml / 12-fl oz jar pickled
   herrings, drained
3 pickled dill cucumbers, thinly
   sliced
2 red dessert apples, cored and
   sliced
1 bunch spring onions, chopped
150 ml / ¼ pint soured cream
½ teaspoon dried dill*

Cut the herrings into thin strips and place in a bowl.

Add the dill cucumbers, apples, spring onions, soured cream and dill and toss well to mix. Spoon into a chilled serving dish.

Cook's Tip

To make chilli 'flowers', make long cuts from the tip of each chilli to within 1 cm / ½ inch of the base. Then use scissors to cut between the existing cuts to make even finer 'petals'. Leave in a bowl of iced water until they open.

Cook's Tip

Make your own soured cream by adding 1 tablespoon lemon juice to 150 ml / ¼ pint single cream. Stir well.

Eggs and Cheese

From breakfast through to your evening dessert, your daily diet probably includes several dishes based on eggs or cheese. Each is satisfying and sustaining, capable of endless variety, and the recipes that follow will show you how to make the most of these two simple ingredients. Non-meat eaters will also enjoy many of these recipes.

201 | Pan-fried Danish Eggs and Bacon

Preparation time
3 minutes

Cooking time
10 minutes

Serves 4

Calories
376 per portion

You will need
225 g / 8 oz streaky bacon
    rashers, rinded
4 large tomatoes, sliced
½ teaspoon mixed dried herbs
1 teaspoon oil
1 tablespoon plain flour
6 tablespoons milk
6 eggs
salt and pepper
1 tablespoon butter
parsley sprigs to garnish

Grill the bacon for 2 minutes and turn the rashers over.

Sprinkle the tomato slices with half the herbs and the oil and grill with the bacon for a further 3 minutes. Remove from the heat and keep warm.

Meanwhile, put the flour in a bowl, pour on the milk, stirring, then beat in the eggs. Add the salt and pepper to taste and the remaining mixed dried herbs.

Melt the butter and pour in the egg mixture, then cook over moderately high heat for 4–5 minutes, lifting the edges occasionally with a spatula.

When set, arrange the bacon rashers on top with the tomatoes. Serve hot, straight from the pan, cut into quarters, garnished with parsley.

202 | Tarragon Omelette

Preparation time
5 minutes

Cooking time
3–4 minutes

Serves 2
as a starter

Calories
258 per portion

You will need
3 eggs
1 tablespoon single cream
1 tablespoon chopped fresh
    tarragon or 1 teaspoon dried
salt and pepper
25 g / 1 oz butter
tarragon sprigs to garnish

Beat together the eggs, cream, tarragon and salt and pepper to taste.

Melt the butter in a frying pan until foaming. Pour in the egg mixture, tilting the pan to cover the base evenly. Cook the omelette gently until almost set, then place under a preheated hot grill for 30 seconds to cook the top.

Garnish with tarragon and cut in half when serving.

Cook's Tip

The butter should be very hot when the eggs are added, then the heat turned down. This is to prevent the butter burning and the eggs from becoming tough.

Cook's Tip

This starter can also be served as a light main course for one person. Complete the meal with a crisp salad and chilled glass of dry white wine.

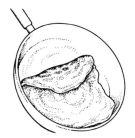

203 | Spanish-style Omelette

Preparation time
20 minutes

Cooking time
15 minutes

Serves 4

Calories
387 per portion

You will need
50 g / 2 oz butter
1 large onion, peeled and sliced
100 g / 4 oz bacon, rinded and chopped
225 g / 8 oz cooked potatoes, peeled and diced
1 red pepper, cored, seeded and chopped
1 green pepper, cored, seeded and chopped
4 eggs, beaten
salt and pepper
1 teaspoon dried marjoram
50 g / 2 oz Cheddar cheese, grated
6 stuffed green olives, sliced
1 teaspoon paprika

Melt the butter and fry the onion and bacon until crisp and lightly browned.

Add the potatoes and peppers and cook for 2 minutes. Beat the eggs with salt and pepper to taste and the marjoram. Pour into the pan and cook until the mixture is almost set.

Sprinkle with the cheese, olives and paprika. Place under a preheated hot grill for 3 minutes until golden. Serve hot, with warm crusty bread and a salad.

Cook's Tip

This colourful omelette is filling enough to make a light meal. Serve it with crusty white bread and a salad with an olive oil and vinegar dressing.

204 | Piperade Tomatoes

Preparation time
10 minutes, plus cooling

Cooking time
20 minutes

Makes 4

Calories
264 per portion

You will need
4 large tomatoes, preferably Mediterranean
50 g / 2 oz butter
2 rashers streaky bacon, rinded and chopped
1 shallot, peeled and finely chopped
1 small red or green pepper, cored, seeded and diced
4 eggs, lightly beaten
salt and pepper
lettuce leaves to serve

Slice the tops off the tomatoes, and reserve as lids. Scoop out the insides of the tomatoes (a grapefruit knife makes this very easy) and chop up the flesh.

Melt 25 g / 1 oz butter and fry the bacon, shallot and pepper for 5 minutes. Add the tomato flesh and simmer for 10 minutes, stirring occasionally, until reduced to a thick purée.

In another pan, melt the remaining butter and pour in the eggs. Cook gently, stirring until the eggs are scrambled. Stir the piperade mixture into the scrambled eggs and add salt and pepper to taste. Leave to cool.

Fill the tomato cases with the cold piperade and replace the lids. Serve on a bed of lettuce.

Cook's Tip

Piperade, sautéed peppers with scrambled eggs, is a classic dish from the Basque region of Spain along the Pyrenees mountains. These Mediterranean-style tomatoes can be served either as a starter or light main course.

205 | Egg and Bean-sprout Tacos

Preparation time
20 minutes

Cooking time
10 minutes

Oven temperature
110C, 225F, Gas ¼

Serves 6

Calories
273 per portion

You will need
6 taco shells
2 tomatoes, sliced, to garnish

For Filling 1
7 eggs
3 tablespoons milk
salt and pepper
1 tablespoon butter
2 tablespoons chopped capers
2 tablespoons chopped fresh
  parsley

For Filling 2
1 tablespoon olive oil
275 g / 10 oz bean-sprouts
1–2 tablespoons soy sauce

Warm the taco shells in the oven while preparing the fillings. Cook both fillings at the same time.

To make Filling 1, whisk together the eggs, milk, salt and pepper to taste. Melt the butter in a small pan and stir the eggs over a low heat to scramble them lightly. When almost ready stir in the capers and parsley.

Meanwhile, to make Filling 2, heat the olive oil until smoking in a frying pan, add the bean-sprouts, and keeping the heat high, stir-fry for 2 minutes, adding the soy sauce, some salt and plenty of black pepper.

Take the taco shells from the oven, spoon the bean-sprout filling on the bottoms, then top with the scrambled egg filling. Serve garnished with tomatoes.

Cook's Tip

Taco shells are deep-fried corn tortillas, popular in Tex-Mex cooking. Look for ready-to-use taco shells in large supermarkets or delicatessens.

206 | Mexican Beanfeast Snacks

Preparation time
10 minutes

Cooking time
10–15 minutes

Makes 4

Calories
455 per portion

You will need
1 × 450-g / 1-lb can baked beans
  in tomato sauce
1–2 teaspoons chilli seasoning
1 canned pimiento, drained and
  finely chopped
½ teaspoon Worcestershire sauce
50 g / 2 oz butter
6 eggs, beaten
salt and pepper
4 slices hot buttered toast
4 tomatoes, thinly sliced
parsley sprigs to garnish

Place the beans in a pan with the chilli seasoning, pimiento and Worcestershire sauce, blending well. Heat until very hot.

Meanwhile, melt the butter. Add the eggs with salt and pepper to taste and cook over a gentle heat until lightly scrambled. Spoon the scrambled egg around the edges of the prepared toast slices.

Spoon the bean mixture into the centre of the egg 'nests'. Top each with tomato slices and garnish with parsley sprigs. Serve at once.

Cook's Tip

If the scrambled eggs are made in the microwave, they will be lighter and fluffier than if made in a pan. You can also omit the butter, greatly reducing the calories.

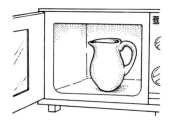

207 | Mumbled Eggs with Pepper

Preparation time
10 minutes

Cooking time
9–11 minutes

Serves 4

Calories
454 per portion

You will need
1 green pepper, halved, cored and seeded
6 slices bread
8 eggs
2 teaspoons prepared mustard
salt and pepper
1 tablespoon butter
100 g / 4 oz full fat soft cheese
2 tablespoons single cream

Place the pepper cut side down and cook under a pre-heated hot grill for 4–5 minutes, until the skin turns black and bubbly. Cool it in water, then peel off the skin and cut lengthways into thin strips.

Toast the bread and cut each slice into four triangles. Remove the crusts if liked.

Beat the eggs and mustard together, and add salt and pepper to taste. Melt the butter, add the egg mixture and stir over moderate heat for 3–4 minutes, until beginning to set. Stir in the cheese and cook for 2 minutes more, until the mixture is softly set. Stir in the cream.

Pile the egg mixture into a dish, arrange the toast round it and criss-cross the pepper strips on top. Serve at once.

208 | Savoury Scramble

Preparation time
5 minutes

Cooking time
5 minutes

Serves 4

Calories
219 per portion

You will need
2 teaspoons oil
2–3 slices lean cooked ham, diced
2 spring onions, chopped
½ red pepper, cored, seeded and finely chopped
4–6 eggs
2 tablespoons milk
1 tablespoon butter
salt and pepper
parsley sprigs to garnish

Heat the oil and lightly fry the ham, onions and red pepper without browning. Set aside.

Lightly whisk the eggs and milk together, then pour into a small saucepan and cook gently, stirring; remove from the heat before the eggs have completely set, while they still look shiny and creamy.

Stir in the butter, salt and pepper to taste, and the cooked mixture. Serve, garnished with parsley.

Cook's Tip

Buy peppers that feel firm and don't have any soft spots, which are indications that the pepper is starting to spoil. Red pepper would also look attractive with this dish. A yellow pepper would taste just as good but the attractive contrast in the dish's presentation wouldn't be as strong.

Cook's Tip

Removing the pan from the heat while the eggs are still creamy prevents them from overcooking. The heat of the pan will be enough for the eggs to finish cooking.

209 | Eggs Mimosa

Preparation time
20 minutes

Cooking time
30 minutes

Serves 6

Calories
322 per portion

You will need
12 hard-boiled eggs, shelled and
    quartered
50 g / 2 oz butter
2 Spanish onions, peeled and
    thinly sliced
50 g / 2 oz plain flour
600 ml / 1 pint milk
salt and pepper
2 tablespoons chopping fresh
    parsley to garnish

Separate the yolks from the whites of the hard-boiled
eggs and pass the yolks through a nylon sieve. Place in
separate bowls, cover and keep warm.

Melt the butter and sweat the onions gently until soft,
but not browned.

Stir in the flour and cook for 2–3 minutes. Remove
from the heat and gradually stir in the milk. Cook, stirring,
until the sauce comes to the boil, then simmer gently for
4–5 minutes. Add salt and pepper to taste.

Arrange the egg whites in the base of a serving dish,
then pour over the sauce. Cover with the sieved egg yolk,
then make a pattern with the parsley to garnish. Serve at
once.

210 | Eggs Stuffed with Peppers

Preparation time
15 minutes

Cooking time
5 minutes

Serves 4
as a starter

Calories
60 per portion

You will need
4 hard-boiled eggs, shelled
1 small red pepper, cored and
    seeded
2 tablespoons olive oil
2 teaspoons capers, well drained
    and finely chopped
4 teaspoons finely chopped fresh
    parsley
2 anchovy fillets, finely chopped
1 teaspoon Dijon mustard
salt and pepper
shredded lettuce to serve

Cut the eggs in half and remove the yolks. Sieve the yolks
into a bowl through a fine nylon sieve.

Plunge the pepper into a pan of boiling salted water
and cook for 5 minutes. Drain and dry with a paper towel.
Cut sixteen strips from the pepper and finely chop the remainder.

Add the chopped pepper to the egg yolks with the olive
oil, capers, parsley, anchovies, mustard and salt and pepper to taste. Mix well.

Spoon the mixture into the egg white halves and top
each with two strips of pepper. Serve the eggs on a bed
of shredded lettuce.

Cook's Tip

*Use the back of a wooden
spoon to push the yolks
through the sieve. If you don't
have a fine nylon sieve, the
egg yolks can be finely
chopped with a sharp knife.*

Cook's Tip

*This versatile recipe is suitable
for serving as a light lunch
dish for two with a salad, or
as part of a buffet for a party.
The stuffed eggs can be
prepared up to six hours in
advance. Cover and chill until
ready to serve.*

211 | Curried Egg Mayonnaise

Preparation time
10–15 minutes

Serves 4
as a starter

Calories
411 per portion

You will need
150 ml / ¼ pint mayonnaise
1 × 225-g / 8-oz can curried beans
   with sultanas
grated rind of ½ lemon
1½ tablespoons lemon juice
75 g / 3 oz cooked chicken,
   skinned and cut into thin strips
salt and pepper
½ crisp lettuce, shredded
4 hard-boiled eggs, shelled and
   halved
paprika to garnish

Mix together the mayonnaise, beans, lemon rind, lemon juice, chicken and salt and pepper to taste.

Place the lettuce on a serving dish and spoon over half the curried beans and chicken mixture. Top with the eggs. Spoon the remaining curried bean mixture over and around the eggs.

Serve garnished with a dusting of paprika.

212 | Easter Egg Salad

Preparation time
15 minutes

Cooking time
10 minutes

Serves 4

Calories
613 per portion

You will need
skins from 2–3 large onions
6–8 eggs
50 g / 2 oz fresh watercress,
   stemmed
300 ml / ½ pint mayonnaise
1 lettuce, shredded
100 g /4 oz bean-sprouts
100 g / 4 oz lumpfish roe to
   garnish (optional)

Pour enough water into a saucepan to hard-boil the eggs. Add the onion skins to the water and bring to the boil. (The water will turn a deep golden colour.) Add the eggs to the pan and simmer for 10 minutes. Remove the eggs and plunge them into cold water.

Shell half of the eggs and return them to the coloured water. Simmer for 2 minutes until they are a rich golden colour. Remove and leave to cool.

Meanwhile, chop the watercress leaves very finely or purée in a liquidizer or food processor. Mix with the mayonnaise and set aside.

To serve, arrange the shredded lettuce and bean-sprouts on a large plate to resemble a bird's nest. Place the hard-boiled eggs on top.

Pour some green mayonnaise over the eggs and serve the rest separately. Garnish with lumpfish roe, if liked.

Cook's Tip

To cook hard-boiled eggs, place the eggs in boiling water and cook for 10 minutes. Remove with a slotted spoon and immediately plunge into cold water. The cold water stops the cooking, prevents overly hard centres and an unattractive grey ring around the yolk.

Cook's Tip

Instead of the watercress, you can also use 50 g / 2 oz sorrel or spinach, cooked, rinsed in cold water and squeezed dry. Alternatively, use frozen chopped spinach, thawed and squeezed dry.

213 | Egg and Cucumber Mousse

Preparation time
20 minutes, plus chilling

Serves 6

Calories
342 per portion

You will need
½ cucumber, peeled and diced
salt
6 hard-boiled eggs, shelled
1 × 450-g / 15-fl oz can jellied consommé, well chilled
300 ml /½ pint double or whipping cream, well chilled
few drops anchovy essence
pepper

For the garnish
cucumber slices
100 g /4 oz peeled cooked prawns
1 tablespoon chopped parsley

Spread out the cucumber pieces on a plate, and sprinkle with salt. Leave in a refrigerator for at least 1 hour. Drain off the water when ready to use.

Place three eggs and half the consommé in a liquidizer or food processor and purée. Pour into a bowl, and repeat the process with the remaining eggs and consommé.

Whip the cream until stiff, then fold into the eggs and consommé mixture together with the cucumber, anchovy essence and salt and pepper to taste. Pour this mixture into a soufflé dish and chill until set.

Garnish with a ring of overlapping cucumber slices round the edge of the dish. Arrange the prawns attractively in the centre and sprinkle with chopped parsley.

Cook's Tip

The secret of making this impressive mousse is to have all the ingredients well chilled. The consommé replaces gelatine as the setting agent.

214 | Blue Cheese Mousse

Preparation time
30 minutes, plus chilling

Serves 4

Calories
766 per portion

You will need
15 g / ½ oz powdered gelatine
3 tablespoons hot water
2 eggs, separated
300 ml / ½ pint double or whipping cream
1 tablespoon Worcestershire sauce
75 g / 3 oz walnut halves, chopped
100 g / 4 oz Danish blue or Roquefort cheese, crumbled

For the garnish
8 walnut halves
1 bunch watercress sprigs
1 small cucumber, thinly sliced

Dissolve the gelatine in the water and leave to cool.

Beat the egg yolks until creamy. Whip the cream until soft peaks form. Whisk the whites until stiff.

Stir the egg yolks, Worcestershire sauce and walnuts into the cheese. When the gelatine is cool, pour it slowly into the mixture, stirring to mix well. Fold in the whipped cream, then the egg whites.

Rinse a 900 ml / 1½ pint mould or bowl in cold water and pour in the cheese mixture. Leave in the refrigerator for at least 2 hours to set and chill.

To serve, unmould the mousse onto a serving plate. Garnish with walnut halves, watercress sprigs and cucumber slices.

Cook's Tip

This can be served as a starter or light main course. To serve in individual portions spoon the mousse mixture into ramekins. Unmould on to individual plates and garnish.

215 | Tangerine and Cottage Cheese 'Flowers'

Preparation time
10 minutes

Makes 4

Calories
199 per portion

You will need
4 large tangerines
50 g / 2 oz shelled hazelnuts with skins, roughly chopped
225 g / 8 oz cottage cheese
50 g / 2 oz sultanas
salt and pepper
1 small lettuce to serve

Cut a cross in the peel at the top of each tangerine extending to within 2.5 cm / 1 inch of the base. Pull back the skin in four sections, leaving the fruit intact. Peel the skin back to make a case resembling the petals of a flower, keeping the skin joined at the base.

Remove the fruit and segment, removing excess pith. Chop into small pieces and place in a bowl. Add the chopped hazelnuts.

Stir in the cottage cheese, sultanas and salt and pepper to taste. Spoon the filling back into the tangerine skin cases. Place the tangerines on individual plates on top of a few lettuce leaves.

216 | Ham and Cottage Cheese Cornets

Preparation time
10 minutes

Serves 4

Calories
228 per portion

You will need
225 g / 8 oz cottage cheese
1 × 225-g / 8-oz can pineapple slices in natural juice, or fresh pineapple
1 small red pepper, cored, seeded and finely chopped
1 stick celery, chopped
salt and pepper
4 large or 8 small slices cooked ham
lettuce leaves to garnish

Put the cottage cheese in a bowl.

Drain the canned pineapple or peel and core the fresh pineapple, then chop. Add to the cottage cheese. Add the red pepper and celery. Season with salt and pepper to taste.

Divide the filling between the slices of ham. Roll each slice in a cornet shape and arrange on a serving dish. Garnish with lettuce leaves.

Cook's Tip

For a more decorative effect, make a cut in each quarter of the peel to form eight 'petals'.

Cook's Tip

Buy thinly sliced pieces of ham so each cornet is easier to roll. To make these even quicker to prepare, make the filling a day ahead and refrigerate, covered.

217 | Pineapple and Cheese Salad Boats

Preparation time
15 minutes

Serves 4

Calories
486 per portion

You will need
1 medium pineapple, about 1 kg / 2 lb
225 g /8 oz Cheddar cheese, cubed
½ cucumber, cut into cubes
50 g / 2 oz brazil nuts, sliced
4 tablespoons French dressing
1 small lettuce, shredded
25 g / 1 oz desiccated coconut, lightly toasted, to garnish

Cut the pineapple into quarters, lengthways, keeping the stalk attached. Cut the flesh away from the skin and cut into cubes. Reserve the skins which will be used as the 'boats'.

Mix the cheese and cucumber with the pineapple and nuts. Pour the French dressing over and toss.

Arrange the pineapples on a serving dish or individual plates. Place some lettuce in each pineapple and pile the pineapple and cheese salad on top. Sprinkle with the cooled toasted coconut. Serve at once.

218 | Avocado and Stilton Toasts

Preparation time
10 minutes

Cooking time
5 minutes

Makes 4

Calories
232 per portion

You will need
4 slices wholemeal bread
1 tablespoon butter
1 large avocado
1 tablespoon lemon juice
pepper
75 g / 3 oz Stilton cheese
8 lettuce leaves and watercress sprigs to garnish

Place the wholemeal bread under a preheated grill and toast on one side. Lightly butter the untoasted side.

Halve, stone and peel the avocado. Cut into quarters, then slice each quarter into four.

Arrange the avocado slices on the buttered sides of the toast and sprinkle with lemon juice and pepper.

Cut the cheese into four thin slices and lay one over the avocado slices on each piece of toast.

Reduce the grill to medium and grill lightly until the cheese is melted. Serve immediately, garnished with lettuce and watercress.

Cook's Tip

Pineapples were originally from Brazil but now year-round supplies are available from all over the world. Buy pineapples that have firm leaves. When a pineapple is ripe, the fruit has full fragrance.

Cook's Tip

For extra flavour, top the avocado slices with crumbled crisp bacon, then add the cheese.

219 | Camembert Puffs with Fruit Conserve

Preparation time
10 minutes, plus chilling

Cooking time
3–4 minutes

Serves 4

Calories
560 per portion

You will need
8 individual wedges Camembert cheese, well chilled
2 tablespoons plain flour
2 eggs, beaten
75 g / 3 oz fresh white breadcrumbs
1–2 teaspoons mixed dried herbs
oil to deep-fry
8 tablespoons gooseberry, damson or cherry conserve to serve

Dust the wedges of cheese with the flour. Dip into the beaten egg and coat in the breadcrumbs mixed with the herbs. Chill about 20 minutes.

Heat the oil in a pan to 190C / 375F or until a cube of bread browns in 30 seconds. Add the coated Camembert wedges and deep-fry for 3–4 minutes until crisp and golden. Drain on paper towels. Serve very hot with the cold fruit conserve.

220 | Cheese Fritters

Preparation time
20 minutes, plus chilling

Cooking time
15 minutes

Serves 4

Calories
467 per portion

You will need
350 g / 12 oz long-grain rice
700 ml / 1¼ pints water
salt and pepper
3 eggs, beaten
100 g / 4 oz Gouda and Cheddar cheese, grated
¼ teaspoon grated nutmeg
3 tablespoons oil

For the sauce
50 g / 2 oz butter
2 large tomatoes, cut into wedges
150 g / 5 oz cottage cheese
2 tablespoons chopped fresh chives
1 tablespoon tomato purée

Place the rice, water and salt in a saucepan and bring to the boil. Stir, then cover and simmer for 15 minutes until tender. Uncover and continue cooking for 2–3 minutes until firmer than usual and all the water has evaporated.

Season with pepper, then cool and lightly beat in the eggs, cheese and nutmeg. Set aside until cool.

Form the rice mixture into round, flat patties, about 2.5 cm / 1 inch thick. Chill for 30 minutes.

To make the sauce, melt the butter and fry the tomatoes for 2 minutes. Add the cottage cheese, chives, tomato purée and season to taste with salt and pepper.

Heat the oil and fry the rice fritters, turning once, for 10 minutes until golden on each side. Cook in batches if necessary, keeping the fritters warm until all are cooked.

Serve hot with the tomato dressing separately.

Cook's Tip

Coating the cheese wedges in the herby breadcrumbs in advance, then chilling helps to set the coating so it doesn't come off during deep-frying. You can coat the cheese several hours ahead, if preferred.

Cook's Tip

It is better to fry the fritters in small batches rather than all at once. Too many items in the pan will lower the fat's temperature. This means the outside will be soggy rather than crispy and fat will enter the fritter.

Pasta and Rice

A busy cook should always have pasta and rice in the storecupboard. These two staple ingredients provide the basis for an infinite variety of easy main courses and side dishes. To save time, make a simple and tasty sauce while pasta is cooking or prepare one-dish meals, such as a rice pilaf or macaroni casserole.

221 | Pasta with Almonds

Preparation time
6 minutes

Cooking time
15–20 minutes

Serves 4

Calories
299 per portion

You will need
225 g /8 oz wholewheat pasta shapes
1 tablespoon oil
1 onion, peeled and finely chopped
1 garlic clove, peeled and crushed
1 × 400-g / 14-oz can chopped tomatoes
50 g /2 oz mushrooms, wiped and finely chopped
2 teaspoons soy sauce
½ green pepper, cored, seeded and finely chopped
1 teaspoon tomato purée
1 teaspoon dried basil
salt and pepper
75 g / 3 oz blanched almonds, roughly ground
finely grated Parmesan cheese to serve

Cook the pasta in boiling salted water until just tender. Drain and keep warm.

Heat the oil and fry the onion for 2 minutes, stirring. Stir in the garlic, then add the tomatoes with their juice, mushrooms, soy sauce, green pepper, tomato purée, basil and salt and pepper to taste. Cook, stirring, for 4 minutes, then sprinkle in the almonds.

Carefully mix the sauce with the pasta. Serve, sprinkled with a little Parmesan cheese.

Cook's Tip

You can quickly make the roughly ground almonds using a food processor. Turn the machine on and off in quick pulses, taking care not to overprocess or you'll end up with a paste.

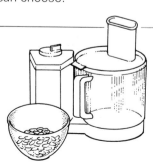

222 | Pasta with Cheese Sauce

Preparation time
5 minutes

Cooking time
8–15 minutes

Serves 4

Calories
498 per portion

You will need
450 g / 1 lb wholewheat tagliatelle
1 tablespoon oil
1 onion, peeled and sliced
1 garlic clove, peeled and crushed
½ green pepper, cored, seeded and finely chopped
50 g / 2 oz mushrooms, wiped and chopped
1 × 400-g / 14-oz can chopped tomatoes
1 tablespoon chopped fresh basil, or ½ tablespoon dried
225 g / 8 oz cottage cheese
salt and pepper
grated Parmesan cheese to serve
nasturtium flowers or basil sprigs to garnish

Cook the tagliatelle in a large pan of boiling salted water until just tender. Drain and keep warm.

Heat the oil and fry the onion for 3 minutes without browning. Add the garlic, green pepper and mushrooms and stir-fry for 30 seconds. Add the tomatoes with their juice and basil, stir well, then bring to the boil and simmer for 30 minutes. Stir in the cottage cheese and heat through gently; do *not* boil. Add salt and pepper to taste.

Place the tagliatelle in a warmed serving dish, pour over the sauce and toss well to mix. Sprinkle with Parmesan cheese and garnish with nasturtium flowers if available or basil.

Cook's Tip

Pasta is cooked when, if you bite a noodle, there is just the slightest resistance in the centre. This is what the Italians call 'al dente'.

223 | Pasta Bows with Walnuts and Cheese

Preparation time
5 minutes

Cooking time
12–15 minutes

Serves 2

Calories
648 per portion

You will need
175 g / 6 oz pasta bows
1 tablespoon olive oil
1 teaspoon lemon juice

For the garnish
25 g / 1 oz walnut halves, roughly chopped
2 teaspoons chopped fresh chives

For the sauce
100 g / 4 oz curd cheese
150 ml / ¼ pint single cream
1 tablespoon grated Parmesan cheese
salt and pepper
1–2 tablespoons milk (optional)

Cook the pasta bows in a large pan of boiling salted water for 6–8 minutes until just tender.

Meanwhile, to make the sauce, gently heat the curd cheese until it forms a thick sauce. Stir in the cream, Parmesan cheese and salt and pepper to taste. Heat, stirring, until smooth and creamy. If it seems a little thick add 1–2 tablespoons milk.

Drain the pasta and mix with the oil and lemon juice. Divide between four dishes. Pour over the sauce and serve, sprinkled with walnuts and chives.

Cook's Tip

Pasta is available in a variety of shapes. In Italian, pasta bows are called farfalle. *Other shapes you can try are* fusilli *(twists),* ruoti *(wheels) and* conchiglie *(sea shells).*

224 | Macaroni with Sausage and Tomato Sauce

Preparation time
20 minutes

Cooking time
20 minutes

Serves 4

Calories
394 per portion

You will need
225 g / 8 oz Italian sausages, skinned
2 tablespoons olive oil for frying
2 garlic cloves, peeled and crushed
2 small onions, peeled and roughly chopped
2 small red peppers, cored, seeded and cubed
750 g / 1½ lb tomatoes, skinned and chopped
2 teaspoons dried oregano
2 tablespoons tomato purée
6 tablespoons Marsala or sherry
salt and pepper
225 g / 8 oz macaroni
25 g / 1 oz butter

Break each sausage into 4 or 5 pieces. Heat the oil and fry the garlic and onions until softened and lightly coloured.

Add the sausages and fry until evenly browned. Add the red peppers, tomatoes, oregano, tomato purée, Marsala or sherry and salt and pepper to taste. Cook gently, uncovered, for 12–15 minutes.

Meanwhile, cook the macaroni in a large pan of salted boiling water for 8–10 minutes until just tender. Drain well and stir in the butter.

Mix together the pasta and sauce and transfer to a warmed serving dish or individual dishes. Serve at once.

Cook's Tip

Prepare the sauce a day ahead. Cool, then cover and chill until the pasta is cooking. Reheat over moderate heat on top of the stove or in a microwave oven.

225 | Seafood Spaghetti

Preparation time
10 minutes

Cooking time
15 minutes

Serves 4

Calories
647 per portion

You will need
4 tablespoons olive oil
4 garlic cloves, peeled and
  crushed
225 g / 8 oz frozen mussels,
  thawed
225 g / 8 oz peeled cooked
  prawns
125 ml / 4 fl oz white wine
salt and pepper
150 ml / ¼ pint double cream
pinch cayenne pepper
350 g / 12 oz spaghetti
2 tablespoons chopped fresh
  parsley

For the garnish
4 unpeeled cooked prawns
quartered lemon slices

Heat 1 tablespoon oil and fry the garlic for 1 minute. Add the mussels, prawns, white wine and salt and pepper to taste, and cook for a further 3 minutes. Stir in the cream and cayenne and heat through.

Meanwhile, cook the spaghetti in a large pan of salted boiling water for 8–10 minutes until just tender.

Drain the spaghetti and mix with the remaining olive oil and the parsley. Serve with the seafood sauce spooned over and garnished with prawns and lemon.

Cook's Tip

Use fresh mussels if they are available instead of frozen. Scrub 225 g / 8 oz mussels well and discard any that are open. Place in a heavy-based pan over a high heat, cover, and cook until the mussels open. Discard any that have not opened. Remove the mussels from the shells and add to the sauce. Sometimes it is possible to buy fresh mussels that have already been cleaned. The mussel shells make an interesting garnish for this dish.

226 | Seafood Pasta Salad

Preparation time
30 minutes

Cooking time
10 minutes

Serves 4

Calories
334 per portion

You will need
175 g / 6 oz pasta twists or other
  shapes
1 avocado, peeled, stoned and
  sliced
2 teaspoons lemon juice
175 g / 6 oz peeled cooked
  prawns
1 × 200-g / 7-oz jar mussels in
  brine, rinsed and drained
3 tomatoes, cut into wedges
50 g / 2 oz button mushrooms,
  wiped and sliced
few whole unpeeled cooked
  prawns to garnish

For the dressing
2 tablespoons mayonnaise
2 tablespoons soured cream
1 teaspoon garlic purée
2 teaspoon chopped chives
salt and pepper

Cook the pasta in boiling salted water for 8–10 minutes until just tender. Drain and cool.

Toss the avocado slices in the lemon juice and add the pasta with the prawns, mussels, tomatoes and mushrooms, mixing gently.

To make the dressing, mix the mayonnaise with the soured cream, garlic purée, chives and salt and pepper.

Fold the dressing into the salad and spoon into a serving dish. Chill lightly, then garnish with prawns.

Cook's Tip

Make your own garlic purée by crushing a clove of garlic with the flat part of a knife blade on a chopping board. If you wish place a piece of greaseproof paper over the board so it does not absorb the garlic's strong smell.

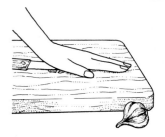

227 | Spinach Noodle Salad

Preparation time
5 minutes, plus cooling

Cooking time
15 minutes

Serves 6

Calories
252 per portion

You will need
225 g / 8 oz green spinach noodles
salt
150 ml / ¼ pint French dressing
small garlic clove, crushed
100 g / 4 oz mushrooms, wiped and thinly sliced
100 g / 4 oz cooked ham, thinly sliced
25 g / 1 oz Parmesan cheese, grated

Cook the noodles in a large pan of boiling salted water for 10–15 minutes until just tender. Drain.

Pour the French dressing into a large bowl and add the garlic and mushrooms and toss well. Add the noodles while still warm and toss again.

Cut the ham into ribbons about the same width as the noodles, add to the salad and toss together.

To serve, transfer to a large bowl and sprinkle with the grated Parmesan cheese.

228 | Pasta, Cucumber and Radish Salad

Preparation time
25 minutes

Serves 4

Calories
163 per portion

You will need
100 g / 4 oz pasta shapes, such as shells, bows or spirals
salt
175 g / 6 oz radishes, sliced
½ cucumber, diced
150 ml / ¼ pint soured cream
pepper
1 Cos lettuce, washed
2 spring onions, finely chopped, to garnish

Cook the pasta in a large pan of boiling salted water for 10 minutes or until just tender. Rinse with cold water and drain.

Put the radishes and cucumber into a bowl and add the pasta.

Stir in the soured cream, adding plenty of black pepper and a little salt. Toss to coat thoroughly.

Arrange the lettuce leaves on a serving dish and spoon the salad into them. Serve, garnished with spring onions.

Cook's Tip

Green spinach noodles get their colour, as the name implies, from the spinach added to the pasta dough. For variety, you can also use red noodles made from beetroots or yellow ones coloured with saffron.

Cook's Tip

This salad makes a complete light meal if served with hot garlic and herb bread. Combine 75 g / 3 oz butter with 3 crushed garlic cloves and 2 tablespoons finely chopped fresh herbs. Slice a French stick at 5 cm / 2 inch intervals without cutting all the way through. Spread the butter mixture in the slashes, then wrap the loaf in foil and bake for 10 minutes at 220C, 425F, Gas 7.

229 | Pasta Pistou Salad

Preparation time
5 minutes

Cooking time
15 minutes

Serves 4
as a side salad

Calories
464 per portion

You will need
225 g / 8 oz pasta such as
  spaghetti, noodles, shell shapes
salt
25 g / 1 oz fresh basil leaves,
  about 4 large sprigs, chopped
25 g / 1 oz Parmesan cheese,
  grated
1 garlic clove, peeled and crushed
6 tablespoons olive oil
1 tablespoon lemon juice
pepper
25 g / 1 oz pine nuts or chopped
  flaked almonds

Cook the pasta in a large pan of boiling salted water for 10–15 minutes until just tender.

Drain and rinse under cold water to cool quickly.

To make the dressing, place the basil in a bowl large enough to hold the pasta. Add the Parmesan, garlic, oil, lemon juice and pepper. Beat until well mixed. Alternatively, place all the dressing ingredients in a liquidizer and blend until smooth.

Stir in the pine nuts or almonds, then add the cold pasta and toss well until it is thoroughly coated. If the pasta absorbs a lot of oil, add another 1–2 tablespoons. This salad is ideal to serve with ham and other cold meats, salamis, and tomatoes in vinaigrette.

230 | Tropical Rice Salad

Preparation time
15 minutes

Serves 4
as a light main salad

Calories
578 per portion

You will need
275 g / 10 oz long-grain brown
  rice, cooked
50 g / 2 oz dried coconut flakes
½ cucumber, cubed
1 small pineapple, peeled, cored
  and cut into 2.5 cm / 1 inch
  pieces
1 tablespoon olive oil
1 teaspoon lemon juice
salt and pepper

For the garnish
2 teaspoons olive oil
50 g / 2 oz whole blanched
  almonds
pineapple leaves

Place the rice, coconut, cucumber and pineapple in a bowl. Add the oil and lemon juice and salt and pepper to taste, then spoon into a serving dish.

Heat the 2 teaspoons of oil and fry the almonds quickly until golden brown.

Scatter the almonds over the salad and garnish with the pineapple leaves. Serve at once.

Cook's Tip

Pistou, also known as pesto, is a classic Italian sauce of basil, Parmesan cheese, garlic, olive oil and pine nuts. If fresh basil isn't available, substitute 2 tablespoons chopped fresh parsley and 1 tablespoon dried basil.

Cook's Tip

Dried coconut flakes are available from health food shops.

231 | Stuffed Tomatoes

Preparation time
20 minutes

Cooking time
20 minutes

Oven temperature
180C, 350F, Gas 4

Serves 2

Calories
371 per portion

You will need
2 large Mediterranean tomatoes
salt

For the stuffing
2 tablespoons oil
75 g / 3 oz button mushrooms,
  wiped and finely chopped
65 g / 2½ oz brown rice, cooked
25 g / 1 oz brazil nuts, roughly
  chopped
25 g / 1 oz currants
1 teaspoon chopped fresh basil, or
  ½ teaspoon dried
pepper
4 tablespoons soured cream and
  watercress sprigs to garnish

Cut the tomatoes in half and scoop out the insides. Sprinkle the shells with salt and place in a baking dish.

To make the stuffing, heat the oil and gently fry the mushrooms for 5 minutes. Stir in the cooked rice, nuts, currants and basil. Add a little salt and plenty of pepper. Spoon the stuffing into the tomato halves.

Cover the dish with foil to keep the stuffing moist and cook for 20 minutes in a preheated oven.

Remove from the oven, top each stuffed tomato with a spoonful of soured cream and garnish with watercress. Serve piping hot.

Cook's Tip

For finger food to serve at a drinks party, use this filling to stuff hollowed-out cherry tomatoes. Serve on a tray lined with lettuce leaves.

232 | Vegetable Pilaf

Preparation time
10 minutes

Cooking time
15 minutes

Serves 4

Calories
309 per portion

You will need
50 g / 2 oz margarine
2 onions, peeled and finely
  chopped
175 g / 6 oz long-grain rice
450–600 ml / ¾–1 pint chicken
  stock
2 carrots, roughly grated
1 cucumber, diced
4 radishes, thinly sliced
1 red or green pepper, cored,
  seeded and finely chopped
salt and pepper
grated Parmesan cheese to serve

Melt the margarine in a large saucepan and fry the onions for 3 minutes until tender. Stir in the rice, then add the stock and bring to the boil. Cover and simmer for 5–10 minutes until tender and most of the liquid absorbed.

Stir in the carrots, cucumber, radishes and pepper and season to taste with salt and pepper.

Continue cooking, uncovered, for 2–3 minutes more until the vegetables are heated through but still crisp.

Serve hot with plenty of grated Parmesan cheese for sprinkling over the top.

Cook's Tip

Using brown rice in this recipe gives it a slight nutty flavour. Brown rice will require an extra 5–10 minutes cooking time. For even more flavour, stir 3 tablespoons of very finely chopped parsley into the mixture before serving.

233 | *Pilaf Rice with Cèpe Mushrooms*

Preparation time
10 minutes, plus soaking

Cooking time
35–40 minutes

Serves 2
as a light main course

Calories
420 per portion

You will need
450 ml / ¾ pint hot chicken stock
½ teaspoon saffron threads
3 tablespoons olive oil
2 shallots, peeled and finely chopped
100 g / 4 oz Italian rice
1 bay leaf
salt and pepper
1 garlic clove, peeled and crushed
100 g / 4 oz cèpe mushrooms, sliced and wiped
2 tablespoons white wine
2 teaspoons chopped fresh chives to garnish

Pour the hot stock over the saffron threads and leave for 30 minutes.

Heat 2 tablespoons olive oil and fry the shallots for 5 minutes until softened. Stir in the rice and stir until all the grains are evenly coated. Add the stock together with the saffron threads, bay leaf and salt and pepper to taste.

Bring to the boil, reduce the heat, cover and cook gently for 30 minutes until the rice is tender and the stock absorbed.

Meanwhile, heat the remaining oil and cook the garlic for 1 minute. Add the cèpe mushrooms and stir until coated. Add the wine and salt and pepper to taste and cook 15–20 minutes until the mushrooms are tender.

Transfer the rice to a warm serving dish and pour the mushrooms over. Serve hot, sprinkled with chives.

Cook's Tip

Cèpes are wild mushrooms available in the autumn. If you can't find any, dried mushrooms have more flavour than ordinary button mushrooms. To use dried mushrooms, soak for 30 minutes in warm water, then squeeze dry and slice.

234 | *Paella*

Preparation time
10 minutes

Cooking time
30 minutes

Serves 6

Calories
583 per portion

You will need
200 g / 7 oz long-grain rice
¼ teaspoon powdered saffron
1 tablespoon oil
1 onion, peeled and thinly sliced
1 garlic clove, peeled and crushed
¼ teaspoon paprika
4 tomatoes, skinned and chopped
1 red pepper, cored, seeded and finely chopped
100 g / 4 oz petit pois, thawed if frozen
4 cooked boneless chicken breasts
2 slices lean cooked ham, diced
100 g / 4 oz peeled cooked prawns
juice of 1 lemon
1 tablespoon chopped fresh parsley
lemon wedges to garnish

Cook the rice in boiling lightly salted water with the saffron until tender. Drain well and keep hot.

Heat the oil and fry the onion, stirring, for 3 minutes. Stir in the garlic, paprika, tomatoes, red pepper and peas and cook, stirring, for 4 minutes. Add the chicken, ham and prawns and heat gently for 3–4 minutes. Stir in the lemon juice and parsley. Mix with the hot rice and turn into a warmed serving dish.

Serve at once, garnished with lemon wedges.

Cook's Tip

Do not be tempted to substitute turmeric for saffron in this Spanish-style dish. Although turmeric will give the rice the characteristic yellow colour, the flavour of the dish will be less delicious.

235 | Fish and Vegetable Rice

Preparation time
8 minutes

Cooking time
12–15 minutes

Serves 4–6

Calories
232 per portion

You will need
225 g / 8 oz haddock fillet
milk
1 tablespoon oil
1 small onion, peeled and finely
    chopped
3 tablespoons water
1 courgette, quartered lengthways
    and chopped
3 mushrooms, wiped and sliced
½ red pepper, cored, seeded and
    finely chopped
½ bunch watercress, stalks
    removed and roughly chopped
1 celery stick, chopped
50 g / 2 oz peeled cooked prawns
150–200 g / 5–7 oz rice, cooked
juice of ½ lemon
salt and pepper

Poach the haddock in milk to cover for 5 minutes or until cooked through and the flesh flakes easily. Drain and flake with a fork, discarding any bones and the skin. Set aside.

Heat the oil and fry the onion for 2 minutes, stirring. Add the water, courgette, mushrooms, red pepper, watercress and celery and stir-fry for 5 minutes.

Add the prawns and continue stir-frying for 1 minute. Add the cooked rice and stir-fry until heated through, then stir in the haddock, lemon juice and salt and pepper to taste. Transfer to warmed serving plates.

236 | Nasi Goreng

Preparation time
15 minutes

Cooking time
30 minutes

Serves 4

Calories
342 per portion

You will need
50 g / 2 oz butter
450 g / 1 lb boned shoulder of
    pork, cut into bite-sized strips
2 onions, peeled and sliced
1 red pepper, seeded and
    chopped
50 g / 2 oz shelled peas
50 g / 2 oz cucumber, chopped
50 g /2 oz carrot, grated
4 tablespoons soy sauce
1 teaspoon curry powder
salt and pepper
225 g / 8 oz long-grain rice,
    cooked and drained
1 egg
1 teaspoon cold water
2 tomatoes, cut into wedges
spring onion curls to garnish

Melt the butter and fry the pork for 5–8 minutes until golden. Add the onions and cook for a further 10 minutes. Add the pepper, peas, cucumber and carrot to the pork mixture and cook for a further 5 minutes. Stir in the soy sauce, curry powder and salt and pepper to taste, blending well. Add the rice, tossing well to mix, and reheat.

Meanwhile, beat the egg with the water and salt and pepper to taste. Melt the butter in a small omelette pan and gently cook the egg until the underside is golden. Turn and brown the other side. Cut in wide strips.

Put the rice mixture on a warmed serving dish and top with a lattice of omelette strips. Garnish with tomato wedges and spring onion curls.

Cook's Tip

Haddock fillets are available smoked and unsmoked. Although this recipe uses the unsmoked variety, a smoked fillet will add extra flavour. When buying smoked fillets, avoid the bright yellow ones: these have been dyed.

Cook's Tip

This is an Indonesian dish that makes an ideal light main course or can be served with a selection of spicy Asian dishes. Add a pinch of five spice powder for a more exotic flavour. The pork can be replaced with shelled **cooked prawns for a seafood version. It will keep warm for 30 minutes after cooking if covered.**

Desserts

With ideas that range from simple fruit salads to luscious desserts, you will always be able to find time to make these tempting desserts and home-baked treats. Many of the recipes help you to make the most of fruit in season. Those that need chilling are a good choice when you have a few minutes to prepare them early in the day, so you can give a hasty dinner a lift with a special dessert.

237 | Chocolate Mousse

Preparation time
25 minutes

Cooking time
5 minutes

Serves 4

Calories
349 per portion

You will need
4–12 rose leaves
175 g / 6 oz plain chocolate, broken into pieces
4 eggs, separated
4 tablespoons strong black coffee
300 ml / ½ pint double or whipping cream
50 g / 2 oz caster sugar

Gently wash the rose leaves and allow them to dry on paper towels.

Place the chocolate in a bowl over a pan of simmering water until melted. Remove from the heat.

Brush the shiny side of the rose leaves lightly with oil. Dip each leaf into the melted chocolate to cover it evenly and leave to set.

Stir the egg yolks and coffee into the chocolate. Whip half the cream with the sugar until stiff and fold into the chocolate mixture.

Whisk the egg whites until stiff, then fold into the chocolate mousse, cutting through until evenly mixed. Pour into individual serving bowls.

Peel the leaves carefully from the chocolate. Whip the remaining cream until stiff and pipe on to the mousses. Decorate with chocolate leaves.

238 | Chocolate Pots with Cherry Brandy

Preparation time
5 minutes, plus overnight chilling

Cooking time
5 minutes, plus chilling

Serves 4

Calories
652 per portion

You will need
200 g / 7 oz bitter chocolate, grated
300 ml / ½ pint single cream
2 eggs
2 tablespoons cherry brandy
dessert biscuits, such as sponge fingers, to serve

Place the chocolate into the bowl of an electric blender or food processor.

Heat the cream just to boiling point and pour over the chocolate. Blend at high speed for a few seconds until smooth.

Break the eggs into the bowl, blend again, then add the cherry brandy and blend until the mixture is smooth.

Pour into four individual serving dishes, cool and then cover and chill overnight. Serve with dessert biscuits.

Cook's Tip

Use a large metal spoon for folding the whipped cream and egg whites into the mousse mixture. Work quickly so you do not knock out too much air, making a heavier dessert.

Cook's Tip

For variety, replace the cherry brandy with kahlùa, a Mexican coffee-flavoured liqueur. Cherry brandy is more like a fruit liqueur than a brandy.

239 | Rum and Chocolate Desserts

Preparation time
25 minutes, plus
overnight chilling

Cooking time
5 minutes

Serves 4

Calories
347 per portion

You will need
butter
225 g / 8 oz Madeira cake or plain
    sponge cake, thinly sliced
4 tablespoons dark rum
225 ml / 8 fl oz strong black coffee
2 tablespoons caster sugar
100 g / 4 oz plain chocolate
2 eggs, separated
300 ml / ½ pint double or
    whipping cream
crystallized fruit slices to decorate

Lightly butter four small bowls or large cups. Line the bowls with cake, cutting the pieces to fit. Reserve enough cake to cover the bowls.

Mix together the rum, coffee and sugar. Sprinkle over the cake in the bowls, reserving a little.

Melt the chocolate in a bowl over simmering water. Remove from the heat, cool slightly and stir in the egg yolks. Whisk the egg whites and fold into the chocolate. Pour into the bowls.

Cover the mixture with the reserved cake and sprinkle with the reserved coffee mixture. Cover and chill overnight.

To serve, whip the cream until stiff. Turn out the desserts onto serving plates and cover with piped rosettes of cream. Decorate the top with crystallized fruit.

Cook's Tip

If you don't have a piping bag, or are in a hurry, spread the whipped cream over the dessert and swirl with the back of a palette knife.

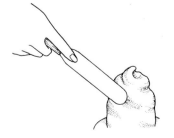

240 | Overnight Chocolate Cake

Preparation time
20 minutes, plus
overnight chilling

Serves 10

Calories
435 per portion

You will need
225 g / 8 oz unsalted butter, diced
225 g / 8 oz plain chocolate,
    broken into pieces
2 eggs
25 g / 1 oz caster sugar
12 oblong semi-sweet biscuits,
    such as Nice or Afternoon Tea
50 g / 2 oz glacé cherries,
    chopped
50 g / 2 oz walnut halves,
    chopped
double cream and glacé lemon or
    orange slices to decorate

Line a 450 g / 1 lb loaf tin with greaseproof paper.

Place the chocolate and butter in a heatproof bowl over a pan of simmering water until melted, stirring occasionally.

Meanwhile, whisk the eggs and sugar together until thick and creamy. Gradually stir this into the melted chocolate.

Spoon a little chocolate mixture into the prepared tin, then add a layer of biscuits, then a layer of cherries and walnuts. Continue layering like this until all the ingredients are used, ending with a chocolate layer.

Cover with cling film and chill for at least 12 hours.

To serve, turn the cake out onto a serving dish. Whip some cream until stiff, then pipe decoratively on the top. Add the glacé fruit slices.

Cook's Tip

This flourless cake is ideal to have on hand for afternoon tea or when friends drop in. For special occasions, sprinkle the biscuits with kirsch, a cherry-flavoured liqueur.

241 | Mocha Soufflé

Preparation time
30 minutes, plus
cooling and setting

Cooking time
6–8 minutes

Serves 8

Calories
344 per portion

You will need
3 teaspoons instant coffee
    granules
3 tablespoons boiling water
3 teaspoons powdered gelatine
100g / 4 oz plain chocolate, broken
    in pieces
5 eggs, separated
150 g / 5 oz caster sugar
300 ml / ½ pint double cream
25 g / 1 oz chocolate vermicelli
150 ml / ¼ pint whipping cream
crystallized rose petals

Dissolve the coffee in the boiling water in a heatproof bowl and leave to cool. Sprinkle the gelatine over the coffee and leave to soften for 5 minutes, then stand the bowl in a pan of simmering water and leave until the gelatine dissolves. Allow to cool, but not set.

Meanwhile, melt the chocolate in a heatproof bowl over a pan of simmering water. Whisk the egg yolks and sugar until creamy and pale. Take the bowl off the pan and whisk in the chocolate until cold. Whisk in the gelatine mixture until combined. Leave the mixture in the refrigerator for 5–10 minutes, or until just beginning to set.

Whisk the egg whites until stiff. Whip the cream until soft peaks form. Fold the egg whites, then the cream into the chocolate mixture. Turn into the prepared dish and smooth. Chill for several hours or overnight.

To serve, peel away the greaseproof paper or foil. Coat the exposed sides of the soufflé with chocolate vermicelli. Decorate the top with 8 swirls of whipped cream with rose petals between.

Cook's Tip

To prepare the soufflé dish, tie a band of double thickness greaseproof paper or foil around the outside of a 1.2 litre / 2 pint soufflé dish to stand 5 cm / 2 inches above the rim.

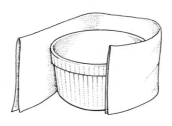

242 | Chestnut Mousse

Preparation time
15 minutes, plus setting

Cooking time
10–15 minutes

Serves 4

Calories
451 per portion

You will need
2 eggs, separated
150 ml / ¼ pint milk
2 teaspoons powdered gelatine
2 tablespoons water
1 × 225-g / 8-oz can sweetened
    chestnut purée
150 ml / ¼ pint double cream
75 ml / 3 fl oz double cream,
    whipped, to decorate

Place the egg yolks and milk in a bowl over a pan of hot water and stir constantly until the mixture thickens and coats the back of a spoon. Do not let the water boil.

Dissolve the gelatine in the water over a gentle heat. Beat the gelatine into the purée with the custard. Set aside to cool slightly.

Whip the cream until soft peaks form, then fold into the chestnut mixture. Whisk the egg whites until stiff, then lightly fold in. Place in four small bowls or a large serving bowl. Chill until set.

Just before serving, top with whipped cream.

Cook's Tip

Add extra flavour to this creamy dessert by replacing 1 tablespoon water with orange juice and stirring the finely grated rind of 1 orange into the chestnut purée.

243 | *Fruity Yogurt Mallow*

Preparation time
10 minutes, plus chilling

Serves 4

Calories
131 per portion

You will need
2 egg whites
2 tablespoons soft light brown
    sugar
300 ml / ½ pint plain yogurt
2 tablespoons mixed dried fruits,
    such as sultanas, raisins,
    chopped dates
1 tablespoon chopped candied
    peel
2 tablespoons chopped hazelnuts
1 large banana, peeled and
    chopped
1 teaspoon lemon juice

Whisk the egg whites until stiff. Gently fold the sugar into the egg whites, then fold in the yogurt.

Fold in the dried fruits, candied peel and most of the nuts, reserving a few to decorate. Toss the banana in the lemon juice and fold this into the mixture.

Divide between four serving glasses and decorate each one with a sprinkling of the reserved nuts. Chill the mallow for a few minutes before serving. It is best made only a short time before the meal.

Cook's Tip

For instant variations, use flavoured yogurts. Try hazelnut, peach or strawberry flavours.

244 | *Stone Cream with Peaches*

Preparation time
15 minutes, plus setting

Cooking time
5 minutes

Serves 4

Calories
270 per portion

You will need
3 teaspoons powdered gelatine
3 tablespoons water
300 ml / ½ pint cold milk
1 tablespoon caster sugar
2 ripe peaches, skinned and sliced
50 g / 2 oz ratafia biscuits
150 ml / ¼ pint double or whipping
    cream
1 egg white
4 ratafia biscuits to decorate

Dissolve the gelatine in the water. Heat the milk and sugar until the sugar has dissolved, then stir in the gelatine. Chill for 30 minutes until cold and starting to set.

Divide the peaches and ratafias between four dessert dishes.

Whip the cream and fold into the milk. Whisk the egg white until stiff, then fold into the cream mixture. Pour over the peaches and ratafias and leave until set. Decorate with ratafias and serve.

Cook's Tip

Stone cream is an old English traditional dessert, usually made with a layer of jam on the bottom. This version uses peaches, but you can also use different-flavoured jams or any fresh soft fruit.

245 | Raspberry Cream

Preparation time
10 minutes

Serves 4

Calories
415 per portion

You will need
300 ml / ½ pint double or
   whipping cream, chilled
50 g / 2 oz caster sugar
1 tablespoon Marsala (optional)
2 egg whites
50 g / 2 oz ratafia biscuits
225 g /8 oz raspberries, thawed if
   frozen

Whip the cream until stiff. Stir in the sugar and the Marsala, if liked.

Whisk the egg whites until stiff, then fold them into the cream.

Just before serving, stir the ratafia biscuits and raspberries into the cream, reserving a few for decoration.

Spoon into four serving glasses or bowls and decorate with the reserved fruit.

246 | Creamy Blackberry Fool

Preparation time
12 minutes, plus
cooling and chilling

Cooking time
15 minutes

Serves 6

Calories
370 per portion

You will need
450 g / 1 lb blackberries, thawed if
   frozen
100 g / 4 oz caster sugar
25 g / 1 oz butter
300 ml / ½ pint whipping cream
1 large jam-filled Swiss roll, sliced
   (optional)

Cook the blackberries with the sugar and butter, covered, over a gentle heat for 15 minutes until the blackberries are tender. Remove from the heat and cool slightly.

Pass the contents of the pan through a sieve into a bowl, pressing well with the back of a wooden spoon to extract as much juice and pulp as possible; discard the seeds. Set aside to cool completely.

Whip the cream until stiff and reserve 2 tablespoons for decoration. Gently fold remainder into the blackberry syrup, using a spatula to mix until evenly blended.

Place slices of Swiss roll, if using, in a glass serving dish, and spoon the blackberry mixture on top. Decorate with the reserved whipped cream.

Cook's Tip

Marsala is a fortified Italian dessert wine with an amber colour. You could just as easily use an orange-flavoured liqueur or brandy. For children, use orange juice.

Cook's Tip

The 'feather' finish is easy to do. Before chilling, pipe parallel lines of reserved cream across the fool's surface, then draw a cocktail stick across in alternate directions.

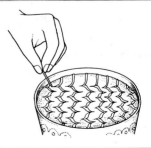

247 | Marbled Gooseberry Fool

Preparation time
12 minutes, plus cooling and chilling

Cooking time
30 minutes

Serves 6

Calories
324 per portion

You will need
750 g / 1½ lb gooseberries, thawed if frozen, topped and tailed
175 g / 6 oz caster sugar
1 teaspoon powdered gelatine
2 tablespoons water
150 ml / ¼ pint whipping cream
1 × 425-g / 15-oz can custard
a few drops green food colouring (optional)

Put the gooseberries and sugar in a pan and heat gently until the sugar has dissolved. Simmer, uncovered, until the fruit forms a thick pulp, stirring occasionally.

Purée the mixture in a liquidizer or food processor, then sieve to remove the seeds. Leave to cool for 30 minutes.

Meanwhile, sprinkle the gelatine over the water in a heatproof basin and leave to soften for 5 minutes. Stand the basin in a pan of hot water until the gelatine has dissolved.

Whip the cream until it forms soft peaks. Stir in the cool, but still liquid, gelatine. Lightly fold in the custard.

Tint the gooseberry purée with green colouring if liked. Put alternate spoonfuls of the gooseberry purée and custard mixture into individual glasses, finishing with the custard. Chill for at least 1 hour before serving.

248 | Grapefruit Mousse

Preparation time
25 minutes, plus chilling and setting

Cooking time
3 minutes

Serves 6

Calories
148 per portion

You will need
4 eggs, separated
100 g / 4 oz caster sugar
3 tablespoons cold water
3 teaspoons powdered gelatine
finely grated rind of 1 grapefruit
150 ml / ¼ pint freshly squeezed grapefruit juice

For the decoration
shredded grapefruit rind
fresh mint sprigs

Whisk egg yolks and sugar in a bowl until the mixture is light and fluffy.

Put the water into a heatproof bowl. Sprinkle the gelatine over the water and leave to soften for 5 minutes. Stand the bowl in a pan of gently simmering water until the gelatine dissolves. Remove from the heat. Stir in the grapefruit rind and juice, then leave to cool but not set.

Add the gelatine mixture in a thin steady stream to the egg and sugar mixture, whisking constantly. Chill for 10 minutes or until it is just beginning to set around the edges.

Whisk the egg whites until stiff, then fold into the grapefruit mixture. Whisk very lightly for a few seconds to give a smooth mixture.

Spoon the mixture into individual glass dishes and leave to set for several hours. To serve, decorate with grapefruit rind and mint.

Cook's Tip

To make the attractive 'marbled' effect, before chilling push the handle of a teaspoon from the top to the base at 2.5 cm / 1 inch intervals all around each serving glass.

Cook's Tip

When grating the grapefruit rind be careful to grate only the outer part known as the zest; this contains the best flavour. If you push too hard, you will include the white pith which will give a bitter taste to the mousse.

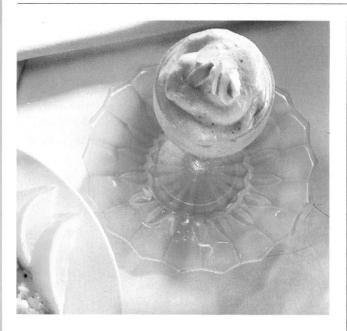

249 | Fresh Fruit Snow

Preparation time
5 minutes

Serves 6

Calories
86 per portion

You will need
450 g / 1 lb raspberries or
   strawberries, hulled
1 tablespoon water
caster sugar
3 egg whites
toasted flaked almonds to
   decorate

Place the fruit and water in a liquidizer or food processor
and purée. Spoon into a basin and sweeten to taste with
the caster sugar.

   Whisk the egg whites until stiff, then sprinkle in 1 tablespoon sugar and whisk again until stiff. Fold into the fruit
purée. Spoon into six individual serving glasses or bowls.
Cover and chill until ready to serve. Decorate with flaked
almonds just before serving.

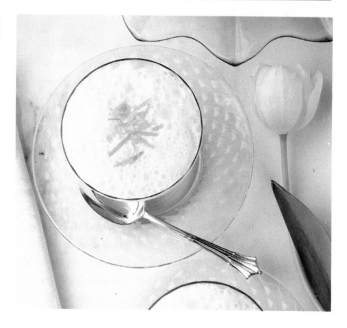

250 | Citrus Syllabub

Preparation time
20 minutes, plus
chilling

Serves 8

Calories
147 per portion

You will need
24 ratafia biscuits
50 g / 2 oz caster sugar
grated rind of 1 orange
grated rind of 1 lemon
juice of ½ orange
juice of ½ lemon
pinch cinnamon
125 ml / ¼ pint dry sherry
600 ml / 1 pint single cream

Arrange three ratafia biscuits in the bases of eight bowls.
   Put the sugar in a large bowl with half the orange and
lemon rinds, all the fruit juices, a pinch of cinnamon and
the sherry. Stir until the sugar has dissolved.
   Add the cream and whisk, preferably with an electric
mixer. As the froth forms, scoop it off and spoon it over
the ratafias. Continue whisking and removing the froth
until all the mixture is used up, then chill the glasses in
the refrigerator.
   To serve, sprinkle each syllabub with the reserved
grated orange and lemon rinds.

Cook's Tip

*Stewed apricots, nectarines,
prunes, apples and peaches
can also be used in this recipe.
Cook the fruit in advance,
then cool and purée. Remove
the fruit from the cooking
liquid with a slotted spoon so
the finished purée is thick.*

Cook's Tip

*This light, frothy dessert
shouldn't be prepared more
than 3 hours before serving or
it will separate. This is a
variation on a popular
medieval dessert and is an
excellent alternative to
heavier, richer desserts.*

251 | Peach Caramels

Preparation time
10 minutes

Cooking time
7 minutes

Serves 4

Calories
415 per portion

You will need
1 tablespoon ground almonds
2–3 drops almond essence
1 tablespoon caster sugar
150 ml / ¼ pint double or whipping
    cream, stiffly whipped
4 large ripe peaches, skinned,
    halved and stoned
2 tablespoons blanched almonds,
    toasted

For the sauce
100 g / 4 oz soft light brown sugar
25 g / 1 oz butter
1 tablespoon milk

Stir the ground almonds, almond essence and caster sugar into the whipped cream. Fill the peach cavities with almond cream, reserving a little for decoration. Sandwich the peach halves together and arrange on a serving dish.

To make the sauce, bring the brown sugar, butter and milk to the boil and simmer over low heat for exactly 7 minutes. Remove from the heat and beat with a wooden spoon for 1 minute until smooth.

Pour the sauce over the peaches in 'waves', so that it does not cover them completely.

When the sauce has cooled (about 3 minutes) spoon or pipe the remaining cream over and scatter over the toasted almonds.

252 | Dried Fruit and Spice Compôte

Preparation time
10 minutes, plus
cooling

Cooking time
15 minutes

Serves 6

Calories
161 per portion

You will need
100 g / 4 oz dried figs
100 g / 4 oz dried apricots
50 g / 2 oz dried apples
100 g / 4 oz dried prunes
50 g / 2 oz raisins
50 g / 2 oz sultanas
50 g / 2 oz currants
1 teaspoon mixed spice
3 tablespoons brandy
150 ml / ¼ pint strong black coffee
150 ml / ¼ pint water

Rinse all the fruit well.

Place all the ingredients in a large saucepan and bring gently to the boil. Simmer for 5–6 minutes.

Spoon the contents of the pan into a large bowl, cover with a tea towel and set aside until cold.

Turn the compôte into a large glass or earthenware pot, cover tightly and place in a cool place for at least 12 hours before using. Stir well before serving.

Cook's Tip

To peel a peach, place in a pan of boiling water for 15 seconds, then drain and remove the skin when cool enough to handle: it should come away easily.

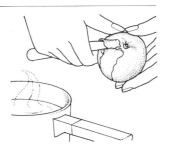

Cook's Tip

For a milder taste, use cold tea rather than the coffee. Do not, however, omit all brandy because that is what acts as the preservative in this recipe.

253 | Blackcurrant Kissel

Preparation time
5 minutes

Cooking time
15 minutes

Serves 4

Calories
231 per portion

You will need
750 g / 1½ lb blackcurrants,
   removed from stems, thawed if
   frozen
75 g / 3 oz soft light brown sugar
4 tablespoons red wine
juice and grated rind of ½ orange
1 tablespoon arrowroot
2 tablespoons caster sugar
4 tablespoons blanched almonds
whipped cream to serve

Cook the blackcurrants with the sugar, wine and orange juice and rind over low heat for 8–10 minutes, or until just tender.

Stir a little of the juice from the fruit into the arrowroot to make a smooth paste. Stir this into the fruit and simmer gently, stirring constantly for 2 minutes until the mixture thickens.

Pour the kissel into a heatproof serving dish and sprinkle with the caster sugar.

Toast the almonds on a baking sheet under a hot grill for 4 minutes, shaking occasionally to brown them evenly.

Decorate the kissel with the almonds. Serve at once or cover and chill. Serve with whipped cream.

254 | Strawberries in Butterscotch Sauce

Preparation time
5 minutes

Cooking time
10 minutes

Serves 4

Calories
433 per portion

You will need
750 g / 1½ lb fresh strawberries,
   hulled

For the sauce
150 g / 5 oz soft light brown sugar
150 g / 5 oz golden syrup
125 ml / 4 fl oz double cream
3–4 drops vanilla essence

To make the sauce, heat the sugar and syrup over a low heat, stirring occasionally, until the sugar has dissolved. Cook for a further 5 minutes.

Remove from the heat and stir in the cream and vanilla essence. Beat for 2 minutes, until the sauce is smooth and glossy.

Serve the strawberries with the sauce, hot or cold.

Cook's Tip

Sprinkling the top of the kissel with caster sugar prevents a skin from forming on the surface. Stir the sugar in before serving.

Cook's Tip

The sauce can be made a day ahead and stored in the refrigerator. If you do this, however, serve the sauce at room temperature because it doesn't reheat well.

255 | *Clementines in Orange Liqueur*

Preparation time
10 minutes, plus cooling

Cooking time
20–25 minutes

Serves 4

Calories
206 per portion

You will need
8 clementines
175 g /6 oz caster sugar
600 ml / 1 pint water
2 tablespoons orange liqueur

Carefully peel the clementines, removing all other bitter white pith.

Put the sugar and water into a large pan and bring to the boil, stirring constantly until the sugar has dissolved.

Add the clementines and return to the boil, then simmer gently for 10 minutes. Leave to cool in the liquid.

Remove the fruit from the pan with a slotted spoon, then boil the syrup until reduced to about 300 ml / ½ pint. Cool the syrup, then stir in the liqueur. Pour over the clementines and serve.

Cook's Tip

Use a small serrated knife to peel the clementines. Cut off the peel in one long strip with a gentle up and down sawing motion, going around the fruit from the top to the bottom.

256 | *Cider Pears with Passion Fruit*

Preparation time
10 minutes, plus chilling

Cooking time
15 minutes

Serves 4

Calories
100 per portion

You will need
4 large pears, peeled, halved and cored
thin strips of lemon rind
2 tablespoons clear honey
300 ml / ½ pint dry cider
4 ripe passion fruit

Place the pear halves in a large pan, cut side up. Add the lemon rind, then pour the honey and cider over. Bring slowly to the boil, cover and lower the heat. Simmer gently for 10 minutes until the pears are tender but not too soft.

Lift the pears from the syrup with a slotted spoon and arrange in serving dishes. Set aside.

Remove the lemon rind, then boil the syrup for 5 minutes. Set aside to cool for a few minutes.

Cut the passion fruit in half, scoop the seeds and flesh into the syrup, stir briefly, then spoon over the pears. Cover, and chill for at least 3 hours before serving.

Cook's Tip

You can use apple juice instead of cider for poaching the pears. Take care not to over-poach the pears, as they will lose their shape and turn to mush.

257 | Poached Pears with Chocolate Sauce

Preparation time
5 minutes

Cooking time
25 minutes

Serves 4

Calories
285 per portion

You will need
450 ml / ¾ pint water
75 g / 3 oz sugar
¼ teaspoon vanilla essence
4 large ripe dessert pears, peeled
100 g / 4 oz plain bitter chocolate, broken into pieces

Bring the water, sugar and vanilla essence to the boil. Add the pears and poach over moderately low heat for 5–10 minutes, turning them occasionally, until they are really tender. Carefully lift the pears from the syrup and keep warm.

Melt the chocolate in the syrup over low heat. Beat the mixture well, then simmer for 10 minutes, until the sauce is thick enough to coat the spoon.

Serve the pears warm, with the sauce separately.

258 | Pears Brûlée

Preparation time
20 minutes, plus cooling and chilling

Cooking time
15 minutes

Serves 4

Calories
350 per portion

You will need
4 ripe pears, peeled, stoned and each cut into 8 pieces
300 ml / ½ pint red wine
75 g / 3 oz soft light brown sugar
2 teaspoons arrowroot or cornflour
2 tablespoons water
300 ml / ½ pint double or whipping cream
150 ml / ¼ pint yogurt
100 g / 4 oz soft light brown sugar

Place the pears, wine and sugar in a large pan and bring slowly to the boil until the sugar has dissolved. Simmer, covered, for 10 minutes until the pears are just tender.

Remove the pears with a slotted spoon and arrange in four small ovenproof dishes.

Boil the wine syrup quickly to reduce to 150 ml / ¼ pint. Blend the arrowroot or cornflour with the water and stir into the syrup. Boil for 1 minute until the syrup clears and thickens.

Spoon some syrup over each dish of pears and chill for 1 hour.

Whip the cream until soft peaks form. Beat the yogurt until smooth, then fold into the cream. Spoon the cream and yogurt onto the pears, covering them completely. Cover and chill for at least 4 hours.

Sprinkle the sugar evenly over each dish and place under a preheated grill for 2 minutes until the sugar is caramelized. Cool and chill again for 2 hours or more before serving.

Cook's Tip

You can also prepare the pears in advance, then chill and serve them cold. Serve with whipped cream and hot or cold chocolate sauce.

Cook's Tip

If you don't have four flameproof dishes, make this dessert in one dish, such as a gratin dish. It must be flameproof so it doesn't crack under the grill.

259 | Mango-stuffed Apples

Preparation time
5 minutes

Cooking time
25–30 minutes

Oven temperature
180C, 350F, Gas 4

Serves 4

Calories
79 per portion

You will need
1 mango
4 cooking apples
soft light brown sugar
150 ml / ¼ pint boiling water
ice cream or custard to serve
(optional)

Peel the mango, then cut the flesh away from the stone and chop. Using an apple corer or small knife, cut out the core of each apple without cutting all the way through.

Cut a line around the middle of each apple and place in a shallow ovenproof dish. Stuff the core cavities tightly with pieces of mango and sprinkle with sugar to taste. Pour the water into the dish .

Bake in a preheated oven for 25–30 minutes until soft. Serve hot with the cooking juice from the dish and ice cream or custard if liked.

260 | Pineapple Rings with Almond Meringue

Preparation time
15 minutes

Cooking time
10 minutes

Makes 8

Calories
142 per portion

You will need
8 slices pineapple, about 1 cm / ½ inch thick, well drained if canned
25 g / 1 oz butter, melted
2 tablespoons dark rum

For the meringue
2 egg whites
100 g / 4 oz soft light brown sugar
50 g / 2 oz ground almonds

Brush the pineapple on one side with half the butter. Place under a preheated hot grill for 4 minutes. Turn over, brush with the remaining butter and grill for a further 3–4 minutes until the fruit is brown and bubbling.

Meanwhile, whisk the egg whites until stiff. Fold in half the sugar and whisk again. Fold in the remaining sugar and the ground almonds.

Sprinkle the fruit with the rum. Divide the meringue mixture between the pineapple rings, rough up the tops with a fork and grill for 2 minutes, or until the meringue is brown. Serve at once.

Cook's Tip

Cutting a line around the middle of each apple prevents the skin from bursting during cooking. This is because the cut allows the steam that builds up to escape.

Cook's Tip

Watch the meringue carefully when cooking. It only takes a second for it to burn.

261 | Blackcurrant Ice Cream

Preparation time
15 minutes, plus freezing

Cooking time
5–10 minutes

Serves 6

Calories
329 per portion

You will need
225 g / 8 oz blackcurrants, removed from stems
100 g / 4 oz caster sugar
3 tablespoons cassis
2 tablespoons water
4 eggs, separated
300 ml / ½ pint double or whipping cream, whipped
sweet biscuits to serve

Boil the blackcurrants with the sugar, cassis and water, stirring well until the sugar has dissolved, then cook until the fruit is soft. Press through a fine nylon sieve to make a thick purée. Cool.

Whisk the egg yolks and blackcurrant purée with the cream.

Whisk the egg whites until stiff, then lightly fold into the mixture. Pour into a rigid container, cover and freeze for at least 2–3 hours. Remove from the freezer 15 minutes before serving, to soften.

262 | Orange Sorbet

Preparation time
20 minutes, plus freezing

Cooking time
8 minutes

Serves 4

Calories
250 per portion

You will need
4 large oranges
100 g / 4 oz granulated sugar
4 tablespoons water
2 egg whites (size 5 or 6)
50 g / 2 oz caster sugar
mint leaves to decorate

Cut off the tops of the oranges and scoop out the flesh, using a teaspoon or grapefruit knife. Do this over a bowl to catch the juice. Wrap the orange cases in cling film and chill until ready for use.

Press the orange pulp and juice through a large sieve. Place the granulated sugar and water in a small pan and slowly bring to the boil, stirring until the sugar is dissolved. Boil for 5 minutes, then stir in the orange pulp and remove from the heat. Set aside to cool.

Pour the orange mixture into a shallow tray and freeze for 2–3 hours until softly frozen.

Whisk the egg whites until stiff, then whisk in the caster sugar. Place the softly frozen orange mixture into a chilled bowl and break down with a fork. Fold in the meringue mixture.

Return the sorbet to the freezer for 2 hours, until frozen.

To serve, spoon the mixture into the orange cases. Decorate with mint leaves.

Cook's Tip

Cassis is blackcurrant-flavoured liqueur made in the Burgundy region of France. If you don't have any handy, substitute undiluted concentrated blackcurrant drink.

Cook's Tip

The sorbet-filled orange shells can be frozen for up to 1 month. Remove from the freezer 15 minutes before serving to soften.

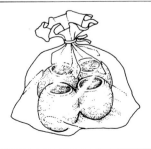

263 | *Champagne Water-Ice*

Preparation time
15 minutes, plus
freezing

Serves 8

Calories
136 per portion

You will need
225 g / 8 oz caster sugar
300 ml / ½ pint water
300 ml / ½ pint champagne
juice of 1 lemon
juice of 1 orange

Dissolve the sugar in the water, then add the champagne and fruit juices. Pour into shallow trays and freeze.

When frozen round the edges but still soft in the centre, tip into a chilled bowl and whisk until smooth. Re-freeze.

Repeat the whisking at intervals until creamy, smooth and white. Serve in chilled bowls or glasses.

Cook's Tip

The Spanish version of champagne is a sparkling wine known as 'cava'. Using cava will give an equally delicious dessert. Set your freezer to its coldest setting 30 minutes before beginning.

264 | *Amaretto Ice Bombe*

Preparation time
15 minutes, plus
freezing

Serves 6

Calories
170 per portion

You will need
50 g / 2 oz Italian macaroons,
    crushed
4 tablespoons Amaretto liqueur
600 ml / 1 pint vanilla ice cream
300 ml / ½ pint double or
    whipping cream
2 crushed macaroons

Place a circle of greaseproof paper in the base of a wetted 600 ml / 1 pint basin. Chill the basin.

Mix together the macaroons and liqueur.

Press a little ice cream over the base of the basin. Spread half the macaroon mixture over the top. Cover with a layer of ice cream, then the remaining macaroon mixture. Spread the remaining ice cream over the top. Place in the freezer for 1 hour.

Whip the cream until stiff. Turn out the bombe onto a chilled plate and cover with cream.

Sprinkle the top with crushed macaroons and return to the freezer for 15 minutes.

Cook's Tip

Amaretto liqueur is an almond-flavoured liqueur from Italy. It is available from most off-licences.

265 | *French-style Strawberry Flan*

Preparation time
20 minutes, plus setting

Serves 6

Calories
169 per portion

You will need
150 g / 5 oz full-fat soft cheese
grated rind of 1 orange
1 tablespoon orange juice
2 tablespoons double cream
1 × 23-cm / 9-inch pre-baked or bought tart shell
6 tablespoons redcurrant jelly
1 tablespoon water
½ tablespoon lemon juice
450 g / 1 lb strawberries, hulled

Whisk together the cheese, orange rind and juice and cream until soft and well blended. Add a little more cream if too thick.

Spoon the cheese mixture into the tart shell and smooth the surface.

Heat the jelly, water and lemon juice together until the jelly has melted. Cool until the consistency of a thick syrup.

Arrange the strawberries over the cheese filling. If the berries are large, halve them and arrange cut-side down. Generously brush the glaze over the fruit and rim of the tart shell. Allow to set, then serve.

Cook's Tip

It's easy to have a supply of baked tart shells on hand because they freeze so well. Blind bake the pastry until crisp, then cool on a wire tray. Wrap each tart shell individually and freeze for up to 6 months. Thaw at room temperature for 1 hour. If desired, recrisp in a 180C, 350F, Gas 4 oven for 10–15 minutes. Cool before filling.

266 | *Fresh Fruit Tartlets*

Preparation time
10 minutes

Cooking time
10 minutes, plus cooling

Oven temperature
230C, 450F, Gas 8

Makes 12

Calories
166 per tartlet

You will need
75 g / 3 oz butter or margarine, diced
175 g / 6 oz plain wholemeal flour
2 tablespoons ground almonds
4 drops almond essence
2 teaspoons soft light brown sugar
2–3 tablespoons water

For the topping
150 ml / ¼ pint double cream
1 teaspoon caster sugar
prepared fresh fruit, such as kiwi fruit, strawberries, raspberries, pineapple, mango or lychees
caster sugar (optional)

To make the pastry, combine the butter, flour, ground almonds and almond essence until the mixture resembles breadcrumbs. Stir in the sugar and enough water to make a moist dough. Sprinkle in a little more flour and knead lightly.

Roll out the pastry on a lightly floured surface, then cut into rounds with a 6 cm / 2½ inch fluted cutter and use to line 12 patty tins.

Bake on the top shelf of a preheated oven for 10 minutes. Cool on a wire rack. Whip the cream with the sugar until stiff peaks form.

Put a heaped teaspoon of cream into each pastry case and top with fruit. Sprinkle with a little sugar if liked.

Cook's Tip

Using ground almonds in the pastry gives a light result that won't be soggy on the bottom of the tartlet case. Use well chilled fat and water for best results.

267 | Lemon and Almond Cake

Preparation time
20 minutes

Cooking time
20–25 minutes

Oven temperature
180C, 350F, Gas 4

Serves 8

Calories
295 per portion

You will need
25 g / 1 oz flaked almonds
100 g / 4 oz butter or margarine,
   softened
100 g / 4 oz soft light brown sugar
2 eggs, beaten
grated rind of 1 lemon
100 g / 4 oz wholemeal self-raising
   flour

For the syrup
75 g / 3 oz caster sugar
3–4 tablespoons fresh lemon juice

Line the base of a round 23 cm / 9 inch sandwich tin with non-stick silicone paper or greased greaseproof paper. Thoroughly grease the sides of the tin. Tip in the almonds and shake so they cling to the sides and base.

Cream the butter and sugar until light and fluffy. Gradually beat in the eggs, 1 tablespoon at a time, then the lemon rind. Fold in the flour until blended, then spoon the mixture into the prepared tin. Smooth the top. Bake for 20–25 minutes, until risen and firm to the touch.

Meanwhile, to prepare the syrup, put the sugar into a bowl and stir in the lemon juice. Leave to stand, stirring occasionally.

Remove the cake from the oven and leave in the tin for 1 minute, then turn out onto a wire tray and peel off the lining paper. Spoon the syrup evenly over the cake, covering the nuts and allowing it to soak in. Serve hot or cold.

Cook's Tip

Place a sheet of greaseproof paper under the wire tray before spooning over the syrup. The paper will catch any drips and make cleaning up easier.

268 | Irish Lace Biscuits

Preparation time
10 minutes

Cooking time
10 minutes

Oven temperature
180C, 350F, Gas 4

Makes 24

Calories
90 per biscuit

You will need
100 g / 4 oz butter, softened
100 g / 4 oz soft brown sugar
25 g / 1 oz self-raising flour, sifted
2 tablespoons milk
100 g / 4 oz rolled oats
1 teaspoon vanilla essence

Cream together the butter and sugar until light and fluffy. Stir in the flour, milk, rolled oats and vanilla essence.

Drop teaspoons of the mixture onto well-greased baking sheets, leaving room for the bisuits to spread. Place in a preheated oven for 10 minutes, then cool on a wire tray. Store in an airtight container until ready to serve.

Cook's Tip

Serve these delicate biscuits with creamy desserts such as mousses and ice cream or on their own. They can also be flavoured with almond essence or grated orange or lemon rind.

269 | *Fruity Bars*

Preparation time
15 minutes, plus chilling

**Makes about
450 g / 1 lb**

Calories
1200 per 450 g / 1 lb

You will need
175 g / 6 oz ready-to-eat dried
  apricots, finely chopped
50 g / 2 oz seedless raisins, finely
  chopped
50 g / 2 oz pecan nuts, finely
  chopped
50 g / 2 oz hazelnuts without
  skins, ground
grated rind of 1 orange
2 dessertspoons clear honey
2–3 dessertspoons lemon juice
icing sugar for dusting

Combine the apricots, raisins, pecans, hazelnuts and orange rind in a small bowl. Add all the honey and 1 dessertspoon of the lemon juice. Stir in the remaining juice gradually until the mixture forms a firm paste.

Turn the mixture onto a piece of baking foil and pat into an oblong shape 2 cm / ¾ inch thick. Wrap the foil round to make a flat packet and refrigerate for 3 hours, until firm.

Remove the foil and cut the bar into small pieces 1 cm / ½ inch wide and 4 cm / 1½ inches long. Dust lightly with icing sugar before serving.

270 | *Pear and Ginger Crumble*

Preparation time
8 minutes

Cooking time
35 minutes

Cooking time
200C, 400F, Gas 6

Serves 4

Calories
414 per portion

You will need
1 kg / 2 lb cooking pears, peeled,
  cored and halved
½ teaspoon ground ginger
soft light brown sugar
single cream to serve (optional)

For the topping
50 g / 2 oz margarine
25 g / 1 oz butter
175 g / 6 oz plain wholemeal flour
1 tablespoon wheat bran
2 tablespoons soft brown sugar

Gently poach the pears in a little water, with the ginger and sugar to taste, for 10–15 minutes or until tender. Remove from the heat and cool in the syrup.

Meanwhile, to make the topping, rub the margarine and butter into the flour until the mixture resembles coarse breadcrumbs. Stir in the bran and sugar.

Using a slotted spoon, arrange the pears in a greased pie dish. Pour over 2 tablespoons of the cooking syrup and cover with the topping, making a hole in the centre.

Bake above the centre of a preheated oven for 15 minutes until browned. Serve hot, with single cream if desired.

Cook's Tip

To remove the skins from hazelnuts, put the nuts under a preheated hot grill until the skins begin to split. Place the nuts in a folded tea towel and rub together until the skins come off.

Cook's Tip

For a crunchier crumble, stir 2 tablespoons chopped walnut halves or blanched almonds into the topping mixture.

271 | *Almond Scones*

Preparation time
15 minutes

Cooking time
10 minutes

Oven temperature
200C, 400F, Gas 6

Makes 10

Calories
123 per scone

You will need
175 g / 6 oz plain flour
½ teaspoon salt
4 teaspoons baking powder
2 tablespoons ground almonds ✗
50 g / 2 oz chilled butter, cut into
chunks
50 g / 2 oz sultanas
150 ml /¼ pint milk
few drops almond essence
milk to glaze

substitute = semolina

Sift the flour, salt and baking powder together in a bowl, then stir in the ground almonds. Rub in the butter until the mixture resembles fine breadcrumbs, then stir in the sultanas.

Make a well in the centre, then pour in the milk and almond essence. Mix lightly until a soft dough is formed.

Turn the dough onto a floured surface and knead gently until smooth. Roll out the dough to 1 cm / ½ inch thick and cut into rounds with a 6 cm / 2½ inch cutter.

Place the scones on a lightly greased baking sheet and brush the tops lightly with milk. Bake in a preheated oven for 7–10 minutes, until the scones are well risen and golden brown. Remove from the oven and cool on a wire tray. Store in an airtight container until ready to use.

272 | *Drop Scones with Bilberry Sauce*

Preparation time
10 minutes

Cooking time
4–6 minutes

Makes about 12

Calories
80 per portion

You will need
100 g /4 oz plain flour
2 teaspoons baking powder
pinch salt
1 egg, beaten
150 ml / ¼ pint milk
oil for greasing
150 ml / ¼ pint soured cream to
serve

For the sauce
225 g / 8 oz bilberries or
blueberries, thawed if frozen
2 tablespoons blackberry jelly
1 teaspoon lemon juice
1 tablespoon sugar (optional)

Sift the flour, baking powder and salt together, then stir in the egg. Gradually pour on the milk, beating constantly until the batter is smooth.

Lightly oil a heavy frying pan, and when hot, drop the batter on to it, 2 teaspoons at a time, well apart.

Cook the scones over moderate heat for 2–3 minutes, or until the surface starts to bubble. Flip them over and cook the other side for 2–3 minutes until golden brown. Keep warm in a folded tea towel.

To make the sauce, stir together the bilberries, fruit jelly and lemon juice and bring to the boil. Simmer for 2 minutes. Sweeten with the sugar, if necessary.

Serve the drop scones warm, and the sauce and soured cream separately.

Cook's Tip

Make these luscious scones extra special by serving with strawberry jam and clotted or whipped cream. Peach jam would also be delicious.

Cook's Tip

Bilberries are small blue berries that grow on moors and in mountain woods. Blueberries are easier to find, being in season from mid-July until October. Frozen ones should be thawed before using in this recipe.

Index

Breast of Chicken
    oven bake MK 6 → 25 to 30'x Brush c̄ oil.
    Shallow Fry ~ gently. hot oil - 15-20' - turn occasionally.
    Grill   - Brush c̄ oil - moderate heat - 15-20' - turn occasionally

___

Sweet + Sour Sausage Meat
    Casserole ~   layer of sausage meat
                 layer of chopped onion
                 layer of sliced Bramley apple
                 layer of (tinned) tomatoes
                    (repeat ad lib)
        Cook c̄. 1 h. (?)